SUPERMAN

DC COMICS

THE LITTLE BOOK OF

™

Paul Levitz

TASCHEN

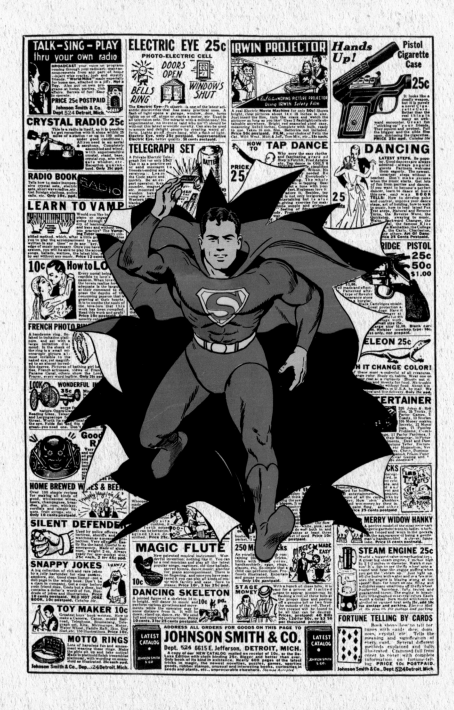

Why Do We Love Superman?   7

¿Por qué amamos a Superman?   11

Pourquoi aimons-nous Superman?   15

The Golden Age   18
1938–1956

The Silver Age   66
1956–1970

The Bronze Age   104
1970–1984

The Dark Age   156
1984–1998

The Modern Age   170
1998–2010

Credits   190

Acknowledgements   192

WHY DO WE LOVE SUPERMAN?

Is it because he fulfills our dream of flying? At the beginning he couldn't. In Cleveland, Jerry Siegel was a student at Glenville High, fascinated by science fiction when he dreamed up the idea of a Superman character with amazing powers. According to legend, he raced to his friend Joe Shuster's house and enlisted the artist in his dream.

The first incarnation of the idea was 1933's "The Reign of the Superman," a prose story by Siegel with illustrations by Shuster. Siegel published it in his own early science-fiction fanzine, *Science Fiction*. The tale explored the consequences of super-human power. The characters and concepts are unrecognizable, but it was part of a development process.

The next version was even more heavily connected to its science-fiction roots: Siegel and Shuster's Superman became the epic prototype of the Super Hero. This was filled out by elements such as a colorful costume Shuster adapted from circus leotards, but he still couldn't fly.

This new Superman was developed as a newspaper strip, and the boys worked up the requisite dailies as samples to send around. It is a truism of all forms of entertainment that the most predictable successes are those closely modeled on previous hits, and the riskiest (though occasionally greatest) are those without a clear precedent. Although *Superman* had elements from other media, it felt like a completely new concept . . . and newspaper syndicate after newspaper syndicate rejected it, often with a complete disbelief that anyone would want to read about a character from a doomed planet who comes to Earth as a hero and disguises himself as a mild-mannered reporter.

SUPERMAN PAINTING

Page 6: *Painting, H. J. Ward, oil on canvas, 45 x 60 in., 1940.*

A SUPERMAN CHRISTMAS

Opposite: *Photograph, unknown, ca. 1940.*

Until editor Vince Sullivan at DC Comics' offices considered what would become *Action Comics* No. 1. The first *Superman* material was bought to fill that hole in *Action*. Indisputably, the cultural ramifications were phenomenal.

Superman was developed as a radio drama, and was flying off shelves as a comic book, comic strip, and toy, but it wasn't until the Fleischer Brothers Studio made a series of theatrical cartoons of the Super Hero that he actually flew.

Is it because we all have a little Clark Kent in us, and wish Lois Lane could see our inner Superman? The brilliant innovation of the Superman–Lois Lane–Clark Kent romantic triangle, which not only evoked the creators' own teenage challenges with Glenville's young women, was an archetype that men and women would respond to for generations. And we're in on the secret, enjoying George Reeves's wink to the viewer on *The Adventures of Superman*, or rooting for a fumbling Christopher Reeve a generation later.

Is it the drama of modern myth? Add in a touch of Moses in the bulrushes reset as a child rocketed from a doomed planet

(named Krypton by Siegel in a nod to its fellow noble gas, helium), and the Super Hero was born.

Superman sales outstripped every other DC Comics title for decades, with even *Lois Lane* outselling *Batman* in the Sixties. Whether you came in on *Super Friends* or *Smallville*, in English or in Urdu, started with his first race against a speeding bullet in 1938 or his best-selling "death" in 1993, you knew his story and you'll recognize the magic captured in this small volume. There's room here to give only a cursory nod to the many brilliant creative people who built on Siegel and Schuster's work, but their magic has kept Superman fresh into a new century.

We love him because he was the original Super Hero, defining the genre for us; because he is our fantasies given life; and because he teaches us, again and again, that with all the power in the universe, the most important moment is what you choose to do: the right thing, every time. Only Superman can do that, and we love him for it.

— *Paul Levitz*

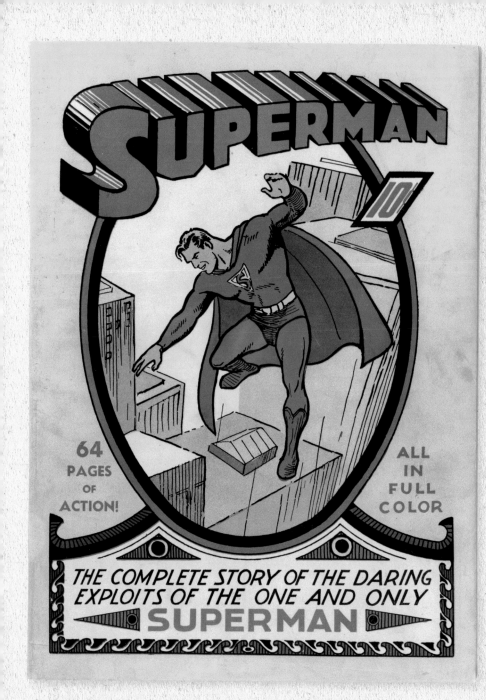

¿POR QUÉ AMAMOS A SUPERMAN?

¿Tal vez porque hace realidad nuestro sueño de volar? Pues al principio no volaba. Jerry Siegel, un joven apasionado de la ciencia ficción, estudiaba en el instituto de Glenville, en Cleveland (Estados Unidos), cuando se le ocurrió la idea de un superhombre con poderes asombrosos. Según la leyenda, corrió a casa de su amigo Joe Shuster y convenció al artista para que se le uniera en aquel sueño.

La primera materialización de la idea fue *The Reign of the Superman* (1933), una historia en prosa de Siegel con ilustraciones de Shuster. Siegel la publicó en su propio fanzine de ciencia ficción, *Science Fiction*. El relato exploraba las consecuencias de los poderes sobrehumanos. Los personajes y los conceptos resultan irreconocibles, pero forma parte de un proceso de evolución.

La siguiente versión presentaba una conexión más estrecha con sus raíces en la ciencia ficción: el Superman de Siegel y Shuster se convirtió en el prototipo épico del superhéroe. Ya aparecen elementos como un colorido traje que Shuster adaptó de las mallas circenses, pero todavía no volaba.

Los jóvenes autores desarrollaron este nuevo Superman como una tira para publicar en el periódico, que fueron enviando a diferentes rotativos. En todas las formas de entretenimiento suele ocurrir que los éxitos más predecibles son aquellos inspirados en éxitos anteriores, mientras que los más arriesgados (y a veces los mejores) son aquellos que no tienen un precedente claro. Si bien *Superman* presentaba elementos de otros medios, parecía un concepto completamente nuevo... Un periódico tras otro lo fueron rechazando, a menudo con un convencimiento total de que nadie tendría interés por leer las historias de un personaje de un planeta condenado que viene a la Tierra como un héroe y se disfraza de amable reportero.

Hasta que el editor Vince Sullivan de DC Comics decidió tenerlo en cuenta para el que sería el número 1 de *Action Comics*. El primer material de Superman se compró para llenar aquel espacio en *Action*, con unas ramificaciones culturales a todas luces fenomenales.

Superman se convirtió en serial radiofónico, y volaba de las estanterías en formato de libro de viñetas, tira cómica o juguete. Pero no voló de verdad hasta que los Fleischer Brothers Studios realizaron una serie de dibujos animados sobre el superhéroe.

¿Tal vez nos gusta porque todos tenemos algo de Clark Kent y deseamos que Lois Lane pueda ver el Superman que llevamos dentro? La brillante innovación del triángulo romántico Superman–Lois Lane–Clark Kent —que no solo evocaba las aventuras adolescentes de los propios creadores con las jóvenes de Glenville— es un arquetipo al que hombres y mujeres responderían durante generaciones. Y ahora que ya conocemos el secreto, disfrutamos del guiño de George Reeves al espectador en la serie *Las aventuras de Superman* o animamos a un titubeante Christopher Reeve una generación después.

¿Es tal vez el drama de un mito moderno? Añadimos un toque de Moisés entre los juncos reeditado como un niño enviado en una nave espacial desde un planeta condenado (bautizado como Krypton por Siegel, en un guiño a otro gas noble, el helio) y así nació el superhéroe.

Las ventas de *Superman* superaron a las de cualquier otro título de DC Comics durante décadas; incluso *Lois Lane* vendió más que *Batman* en la década de 1960. Tanto si entró en contacto con él en la serie *Super Friends* o en *Smallville*, en inglés o en urdu, en su primera carrera contra una bala a toda velocidad en 1938 o en su «muerte» superventas en 1993, ya conoce su historia y sin duda reconocerá la magia recogida en este pequeño volumen. Aquí apenas tenemos espacio para un rápido reconocimiento a las muchas mentes creativas y brillantes que han desarrollado la obra de Siegel y Shuster, cuya magia ha llevado a Superman en plena forma a un nuevo siglo.

Lo amamos porque es el superhéroe original, el que definió el género para nosotros, porque hace realidad nuestras fantasías, y porque nos enseña una y otra vez que, con todo el poder del universo, el instante más importante es aquel en el que decides qué hacer: siempre lo correcto. Solo Superman puede hacerlo, y por eso lo amamos.

— *Paul Levitz*

POURQUOI AIMONS-NOUS SUPERMAN ?

Est-ce parce qu'il réalise notre rêve de voler ? Au départ, il ne volait pas. Le passionné de science-fiction Jerry Siegel fréquentait le lycée Glenville High de Cleveland quand il vit en rêve un personnage de surhomme doté de pouvoirs extraordinaires. La légende veut qu'il se soit précipité chez son ami Joe Shuster pour faire participer le jeune artiste à son rêve.

Cette idée s'incarne pour la première fois en 1933 avec « The Reign of the Superman », une histoire en prose écrite par Siegel et illustrée par Shuster. Siegel la publie dans son propre fanzine de science-fiction, *Science Fiction*. L'intrigue s'attache aux conséquences d'un pouvoir surhumain. Les personnages et les concepts sont méconnaissables, mais ces divergences ont participé au processus de développement du projet.

La version suivante est liée de façon plus intense encore à la science-fiction où elle plonge ses racines : le Superman de Siegel et Shuster devient le prototype épique du superhéros. Le personnage s'étoffe, notamment grâce à un costume haut en couleur pour lequel Shuster s'est inspiré des justaucorps de cirque, mais il ne vole toujours pas.

Ce nouveau Superman est décliné en strip de presse et les garçons utilisent les histoires quotidiennes requises comme échantillons qu'ils font circuler chez les éditeurs. C'est un truisme pour toutes les formes de divertissement : les succès les plus prévisibles sont ceux qui s'inspirent le plus de succès précédents, tandis que les plus risqués (bien que parfois les plus beaux) sont ceux qui n'ont pas de précédent évident. Bien que *Superman* puise certains éléments dans d'autres domaines culturels, il donnait l'impression d'être un concept totalement nouveau... que les éditeurs rejetèrent les uns après les autres, non sans exprimer leur incrédulité totale sur l'existence d'un lectorat potentiellement intéressé par les aventures d'un personnage tombé d'une planète maudite sur la Terre pour devenir un héros déguisé en reporter mollasson.

Les opinions changèrent quand l'éditeur de DC Comics Vince Sulivan commença à réfléchir à ce que deviendrait le numéro inaugural d'*Action Comics*. Il acheta la première histoire de Superman pour combler un vide dans la maquette. Un choix dont les ramifications culturelles s'avèreront indubitablement phénoménales.

Superman se décline en pièce radiophonique et s'arrache en bande dessinée, en comic strip ou en jouet, mais il ne prend son premier envol que dans la série de dessins animés produits par le Fleischer Brothers Studio.

Est-ce que nous l'aimons parce que nous sommes tous un peu comme Clark Kent et que nous souhaitons qu'une Lois Lane reconnaisse le Superman qui sommeille en nous ? L'innovation magistrale que représente le triangle amoureux Superman – Lois Lane – Clark Kent, qui fait notamment référence aux rapports compliqués des deux créateurs encore adolescents avec la gent féminine de Glenville, constitue un archétype auquel plusieurs générations d'hommes et de femmes s'identifieront. Et nous sommes mis dans le secret, capables d'apprécier à sa juste valeur le clin d'œil de George Reeves aux spectateurs dans *The Adventures of Superman*, puis de défendre un Christopher Reeve légèrement tâtonnant une génération plus tard.

Est-ce parce qu'il exprime le drame du mythe moderne ? Ajoutez une pincée de Moïse flottant entre les joncs, que rappelle si clairement cet autre tout jeune enfant placé dans une navette pour être sauvé d'une planète condamnée (que Siegel baptise Krypton en référence à un autre gaz noble, l'hélium), et un superhéros est né.

Les ventes de Superman ont dépassé celles de tous les autres titres DC dès le début et pendant plusieurs dizaines d'années – même *Lois Lane* se vendit mieux que *Batman* dans les années 1960. Que vous l'ayez découvert dans *Super Friends* ou dans *Smallville*, en anglais ou en urdu, lors de sa première course contre une balle en pleine vitesse en 1938 ou de son épisode le plus vendu, celui de sa mort, en 1993, son histoire vous est familière et vous reconnaîtrez la magie qui le caractérise dans ce petit volume. Nous avons juste assez de place pour un rapide salut aux très nombreuses personnes créatives et brillantes qui ont fait fructifier le travail de Siegel et Schuster, et dont le talent a conservé à Superman toute sa magie et toute sa fraîcheur d'un siècle à l'autre.

Nous l'aimons parce qu'il a été le premier superhéros, qu'il a définit un genre ; parce qu'il a donné vie à nos fantasmes, et parce qu'il nous enseigne, encore et encore, que même doté de tout le pouvoir de l'univers, c'est ce que vous choisissez de faire à chaque instant qui est important : agir pour le bien, à chaque fois. Seul Superman est capable de ça, et c'est pour cela que nous l'aimons.

— *Paul Levitz*

THE GOLDEN AGE

1938–1956

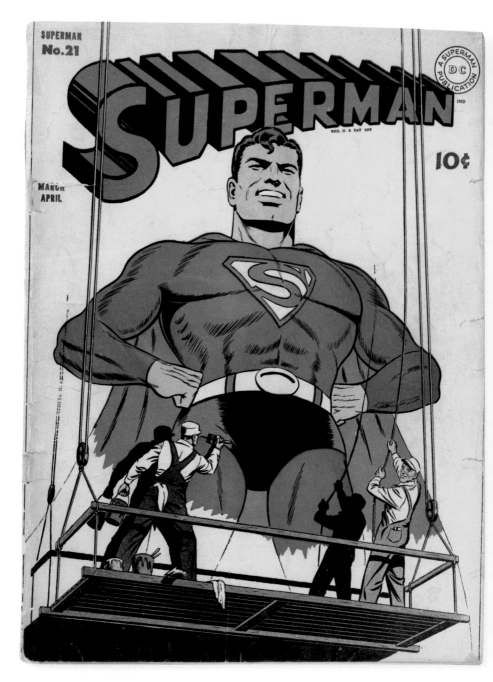

ACTION COMICS No. 1

Previous spread: *Cover art, Joe Shuster, June 1938.*

SUPERMAN No. 21

Opposite: *Cover art, Jack Burnley, March – April 1943.* Originally a two-man operation, Superman soon welcomed a satellite team of creators who were charged with chronicling his adventures. Although Jerry Siegel scripted all the Superman stories in this issue, artists Ed Dobrotka, Leo Nowak, Pete Riss, George Roussos, and John Sikela joined Joe Shuster in drawing it.

SUPERMAN No. 16

Above: *Cover art, Fred Ray, May – June 1942.* The real Metropolis, in Illinois, has its own Superman statue with the simple invocation "Truth — Justice — The American Way." The town hosts an annual Superman celebration.

SUPERMAN No. 20

Above: *Interior, "Superman's Secret Revealed"; script, Jerry Siegel; pencils, Ed Dobrotka; inks, John Sikela. January – February 1943.* "In the silent films, my hero was Douglas Fairbanks Sr., who was very agile and athletic.... He had a stance which I often used in drawing Superman. You'll see in many of his roles — including Robin Hood — that he always stood with his hands on his hips and his feet spread apart, laughing — taking nothing seriously. Clark Kent, I suppose, had a little bit of [bespectacled comic actor] Harold Lloyd in him." —Joe Shuster

ACTION COMICS No. 29

Opposite: *Interior, "Superman"; script, Jerry Siegel; pencils and inks, Jack Burnley. October 1940.* The early Superman was very much a populist crusader, as in this story, in which he intervenes on behalf of elderly citizens victimized by an insurance scam linked to a pharmacy.

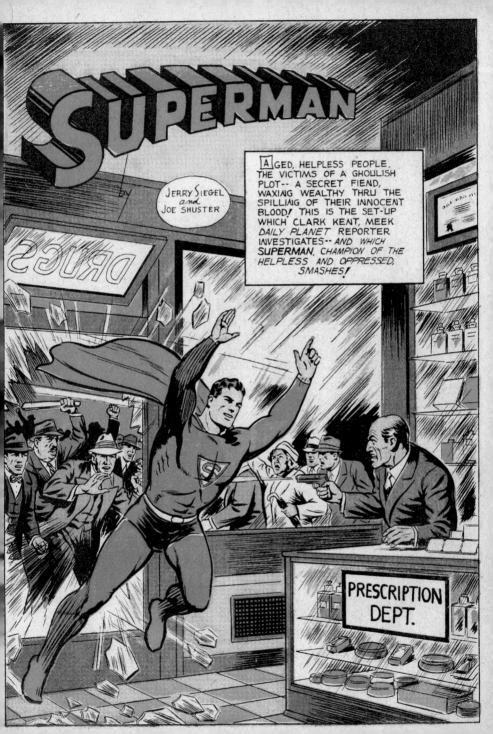

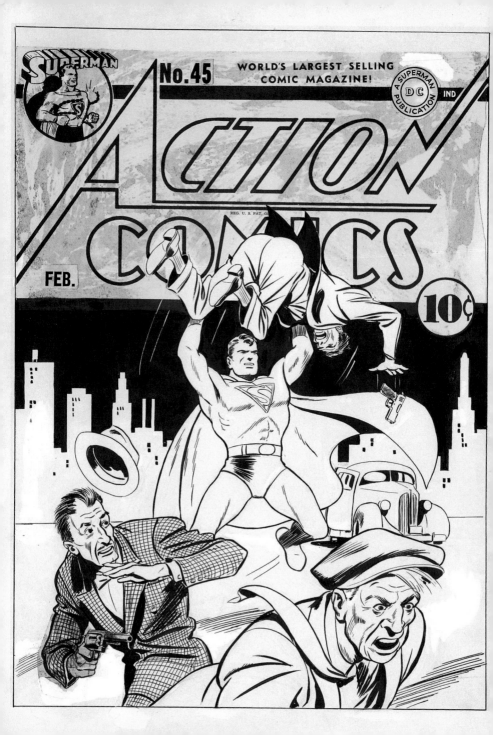

ACTION COMICS No. 45

Opposite: *Original cover art, Fred Ray, February 1942*. The early Superman could be a fearsome presence, even killing a handful of early opponents.

ACTION COMICS No. 50

Above: *Cover art, Fred Ray, July 1942*.

ACTION COMICS No. 13

Above left: *Cover art, Joe Shuster, June 1939.*

ACTION COMICS No. 23

Above right: *Cover art, Joe Shuster and Paul Cassidy, April 1940.*
The generic rescue scene of this issue's cover gave no hint that
a decades-old rivalry was about to begin. Intervening in the war
between the countries of Toran and Galonia, Superman fought
the scientific weaponry of a red-haired scientist named Luthor.

ACTION COMICS No. 89

Opposite: *Cover art, Wayne Boring and Stan Kaye, October 1945.*
Debates over which background colors would make covers
more noticeable and sell better raged among editors and art
directors throughout the nearly 50 years comics were distributed exclusively on newsstands. One truism that seems
to have been universally accepted was that rainbow patterns
were sure-fire attention-getters, as this cover attests. In this
early Superman experiment, color is used to create a hypnotic
effect to which even the Man of Steel seems vulnerable.

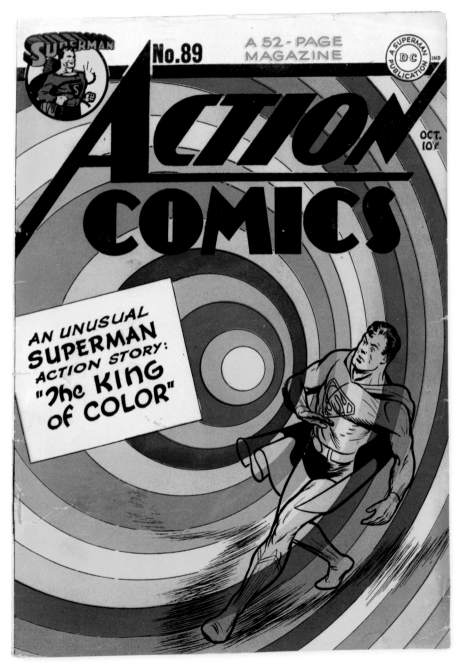

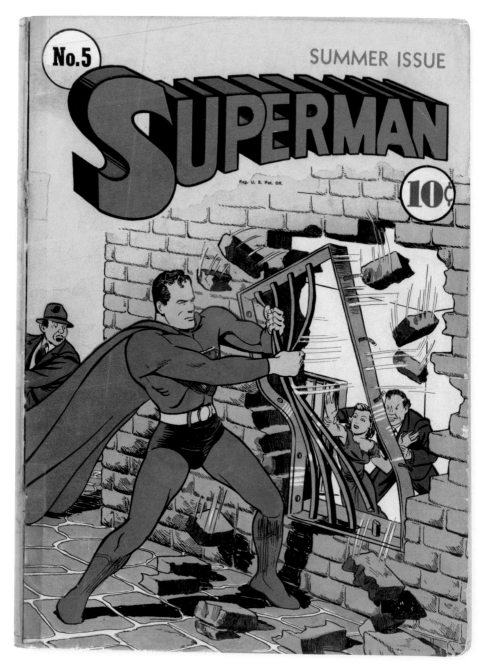

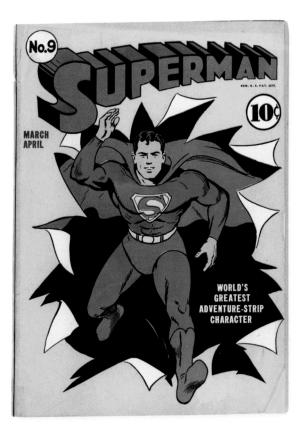

SUPERMAN No. 5

Opposite: *Cover art, Wayne Boring and Paul Lauretta, summer 1940.* "Back then, comic books were the stepchild of the publishing industry. Mostly, they were looked down on, except by their millions of ardent readers." —Jerry Siegel

SUPERMAN No. 9

Above: *Cover art, Fred Ray, March–April 1941.* Renowned for his Golden Age Super Hero covers, Fred Ray was also a respected Revolutionary War historian. He spent more than two decades drawing DC's Tomahawk feature, which was set in that era, and produced a number of historical comics pamphlets.

SUPERMAN TEST REEL IMAGE

Following spread: *Animation cel; producer, Max Fleischer; director, Dave Fleischer. 1940.*

MERRIE MELODIES SUPERMAN SPOOF

Above: *Animation stills, "Goofy Groceries"; director, Robert Clampett; March 29, 1941.* Superman quickly became a popular target for parody, beginning with this animated sequence from Warner Bros. Other cartoon jabs came in Terrytoons' 1942 *The Mouse of Tomorrow* and a 1943 Bugs Bunny episode entitled *Super Rabbit*.

SUPERMAN IS HERE!

Opposite: *Poster, Max Fleischer's* Superman *animated shorts, Fleischer Studios and Paramount Pictures, 1941.* "The Fleischer Superman cartoons were the first Hollywood cartoons not based on fairy tales or revolving around slapstick sight gags. They were the first to tell serious science-fiction stories in a strong visual style combining the art of Joe Shuster's comics with graphics straight off a pulp magazine cover. They are fast paced and exciting, and as far as I'm concerned, all the Super Hero movies of today — live action or animated — owe a tip of the hat to these remarkable cartoons." — Jerry Beck

FLEISCHER STUDIOS SUPERMAN

Opposite: *Layout drawing and animation cel detail,* Superman *(first episode); producer, Max Fleischer; director, Dave Fleischer; animation, Steve Muffati and Frank Endres. 1941.*

MACY'S THANKSGIVING DAY PARADE

Below: *Superman balloon, Times Square, New York, New York, November 21, 1940.* The Macy's Thanksgiving Day Parade in New York began featuring balloon characters in 1927 with Felix the Cat, but Superman's debut in 1940 took him to new heights. Broadcast on radio at that time, the parade later became a television staple of the American family holiday as the turkey slowly roasted.

SUPERMAN No. 7

Opposite: *Interior, "Superman"; script, Jerry Siegel; pencils and inks, Wayne Boring. November–December 1940.* "I liked Joe Shuster's Superman. It was an awkward style, it wasn't a great style, but he told a story very well. When you saw his Superman pick up an automobile, it looked great. I mean, look at this little man picking up an automobile—you know, fantastic. But today, when Superman picks up an automobile, you say, 'Well, that's no big trick. Look at the muscles on this guy. I mean, he could probably pick up two automobiles.'"
—Sheldon Moldoff

ACTION COMICS No. 6

Above: *Interiors, "Superman"; script, Jerry Siegel; pencils and inks, Joe Shuster. November 1938.* Superman's licensing potential was apparent to Jerry Siegel almost from the start, as seen in these examples cooked up by a crook claiming to be the Man of Steel's agent. DC quickly launched Superman Inc. as a licensing arm—later to grow into Licensing Corporation of America.

ACTION COMICS No. 108

Above left: *Cover art, Jack Burnley and Stan Kaye, May 1947.*
Most of Jack Burnley's covers derived from rough sketches
drawn by editor Whitney Ellsworth. "I wasn't interested in
thinking up ideas for covers," the artist explained.

ACTION COMICS No. 61

Above right: *Cover art, Jack Burnley, June 1943.* "Fire can't
burn him, knives can't cut him, bullets can't hurt him....In
fact, there's nothing known to man that can harm even a
hair on Superman's head!" —Caption in *Superman* No.107,
August 1956

SUPERMAN No. 24

Opposite: *Cover art, Jack Burnley, September – October 1943.*

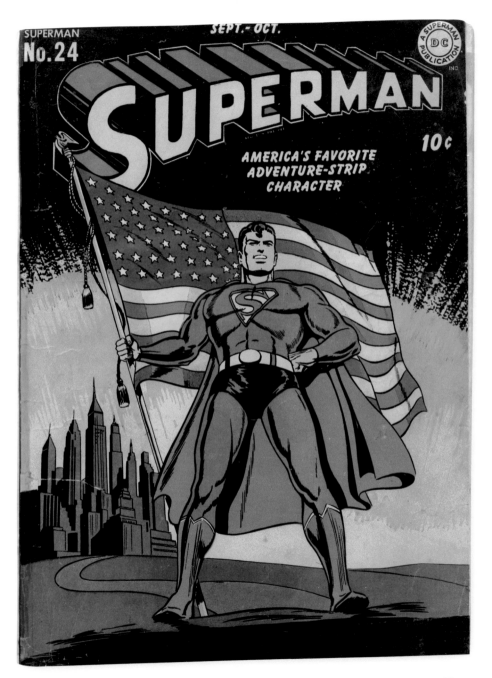

O LOBINHO No. 10

Above: *Cover art, artist unknown, 1941*. Journalist Adolfo Aizen spearheaded the publication of translated U.S. comics in Brazil in the 1930s and 1940s in inexpensive magazines like this.

SUPERMAN ANIMATED SHORTS

Opposite: *Poster, Swedish release, 1941*.

ADVENTURES OF SUPERMAN

Opposite: *Film still, Superman drops from the sky, 1950s.* Among the tricks used to create the illusion of flight was the use of wires to depict Superman in the air and a stunt that showed him dropping to the ground on his feet as if landing.

SUPERMAN AND THE MOLE MEN

Above: *Lobby card, with George Reeves and Phyllis Coates, 1951.*

SUPERMAN IN EXILE

Opposite: *Movie poster, 20th Century Fox, 1954.* This one-sheet promotes one of five "features" that were actually compilations of episodes from the TV series' second season. The episode titles are shown in the blue boxes with white text.

SUPER PUP

Above: *Film stills, Billy Curtis (as Superpup), 1958.* Conceived by *Adventures of Superman* producer Whitney Ellsworth, *Adventures of Superpup* reimagined the original show with actors dressed as canines. Billy Curtis portrayed Superpup and Bark Bent while *Daily Bugle* editor Terry Bite and reporter Pamela Poodle were portrayed by Angelo Rossitto and Ruth Delfino, respectively. The series never went beyond the pilot stage.

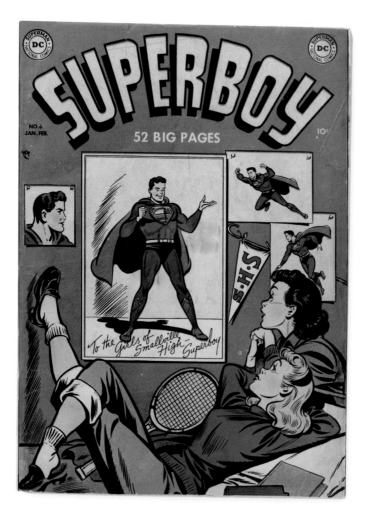

SUPERBOY No. 6

Above: *Cover art, Al Plastino, January – February 1950*. Even as Super Hero comic books were dying on the vine, *Superboy* was a surprise hit. It owed a share of its success to the fact that its teenage hero's interaction with bullies and girls had relevance to kids, but the fact that the feature was about the adventures of Superman as a boy surely didn't hurt.

SUPERBOY No. 1

Opposite: *Cover art, Wayne Boring and Stan Kaye, March – April 1949*.

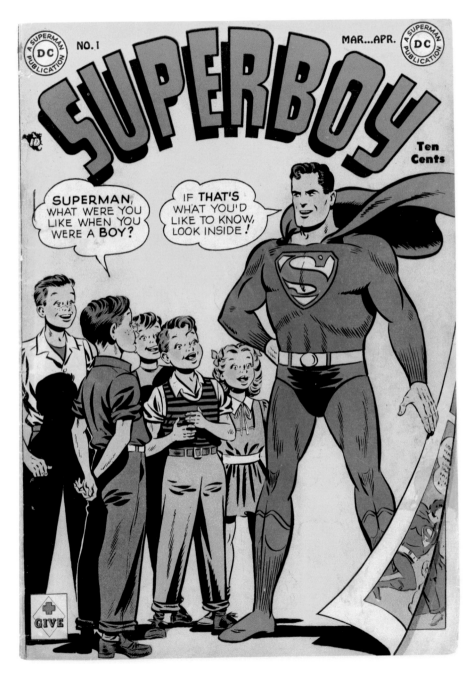

COMIC BOOK WINDOW DISPLAY

Below: *Photograph, location unknown, 1948.*

NICKEL COMICS STAND

Opposite: *Photograph, ca. 1947.* When comic book publishers spoke of their circulation, they often boosted the numbers by including pass-along readers — kids who read copies purchased by their friends. The pass-along effect was enhanced further through used book stores that sold old comic books for five cents, half the price of a new one.

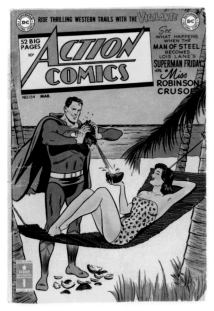

ACTION COMICS No. 33

Opposite: *Interior, "Superman"; script, Jerry Siegel; pencils and inks, Jack Burnley. February 1941.* Superman's rescue of a drowning Lois Lane is one of the most vivid story pages of the Golden Age, a tribute to Jack Burnley's design skill and the realistic character work he honed while working as a sports cartoonist.

SUPERMAN No. 67

Above left: *Cover art, Al Plastino, November–December 1950.* Lois doesn't think real-life singer Perry Como can hold a candle to Superman until she watches him perform. Realizing that he's disrupted the natural order of things, Como conspires to return the love-struck girl reporter's attention to the Man of Steel.

ACTION COMICS No. 154

Above right: *Cover art, Win Mortimer, March 1951.* What could be more romantic for a couple than being stranded together on a deserted island? In truth, the story behind the cover is more a battle of the sexes, with Clark Kent and Lois Lane engaging in a contest to determine which of them can better survive on the atoll.

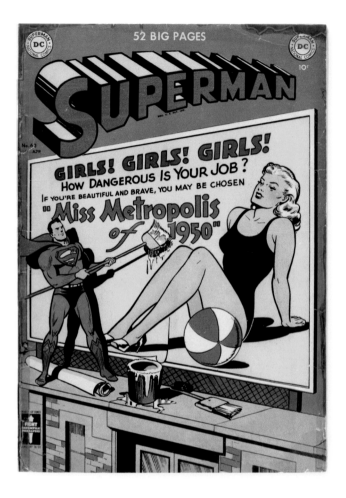

SUPERMAN No. 63

Above: *Cover art, Al Plastino, March – April 1950.* Beauty contests with women in bathing suits date back to 1921, but the competition in this story looked for females who also worked in dangerous professions. The finalists consisted of a cowgirl, a stuntwoman, a chemical engineer, and a trapeze artist.

ACTION COMICS No. 156

Opposite: *Cover art, Al Plastino, May 1951.*

SUPERMAN IN COLOR AD

Following spread: *Advertising art, Joe Shuster, 1939.*

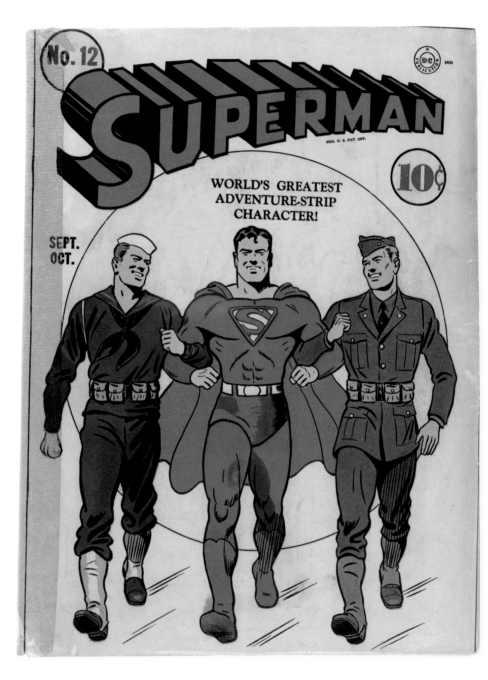

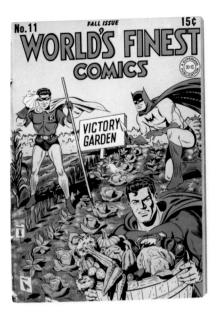

SUPERMAN No. 12

Opposite: *Cover art, Fred Ray, September–October 1941.* Many
DC heroes waved the flag figuratively if not literally as the
shadow of war fell over the United States. *All-American
Comics'* Hop Harrigan was already a renowned civilian pilot
and put his experience to good use as part of the U.S. Army
Air Corps starting in 1942.

WORLD'S FINEST COMICS No. 11

Above left: *Cover art, Jack Burnley, autumn 1943.* Another
war initiative was the victory garden. As public food suppliers
struggled to keep up with the additional demands necessary
to feed soldiers, the general public was encouraged to grow
their own vegetables in private gardens to reduce the strain.
As with the sale of war bonds, the cultivation of victory gardens helped give citizens feelings of self-worth and patriotism.
Superman, Batman, and Robin were happy to do their part.

ACTION COMICS No. 58

Above right: *Cover art, Jack Burnley, March 1943.*

SUPERMAN HOLIDAY CARD
Above: *World War II–era card, 1940s.*

ACTION COMICS No. 101
Opposite: *Cover art, Win Mortimer, October 1946.* Superman's postwar embrace of the Atomic Age was preceded by an innocent early-1945 story in his newspaper comic strip that caught the eye of the government. "The War Department stepped in to prevent Superman from pursuing his investigation of nuclear physics any further. 'Superman was denied,' wrote Louis N. Ridenour in *Fortune* (November 1945), 'a proposed bombardment of 3 million volt electrons from a cyclotron.'"
— John Lansdale, Jr. *Harper's*, 1945

SUPERMAN No. 89

Opposite: *Cover art, Curt Swan and Stan Kaye, May 1954.*
Few artists were as closely linked to Superman as Curt
Swan, whose realistic perspective on the Man of Steel and
his world brought a comforting humanity and accessibility to
the character. While a regular artist on offshoot features like
Superboy and Jimmy Olsen, Swan drew only a handful of
Superman stories during the 1950s. Instead, artists such as
Wayne Boring and Al Plastino maintained the exaggerated
visual style of the Man of Steel in his own comics while
Swan projected a more contemporary image of the hero
by drawing the covers.

ACTION COMICS No. 107

Below: *Cover art, Jack Burnley and Stan Kaye, April 1947.*

SUPERMAN No. 6

Opposite: *Interior, "Super Strength"; script, Jerry Siegel; pencils and inks, Jack Burnley. September – October 1940.* No kid could really become Superman through these exercises any more than they could gain the strength of Popeye through devouring spinach. Still, the intentions of pages like these (a variation of which appeared in *Batman*) were good.

ACTION COMICS No. 92

Above left: *Cover art, Jack Burnley and Stan Kaye, January 1946.* In contrast to the more cartoony versions of Superman by other artists, Jack Burnley's work stood out with its more realistic depictions of the human figure.

SUPERMAN No. 45

Above right: *Cover art, Jack Burnley and George Roussos, March – April 1947.* "Superman burrows faster and more silently than any excavating machine ever invented by man," declares *Superman* No. 11. It seems inevitable that the Man of Steel would eventually be used to illustrate the cliché of digging a hole to China, a gag also used in a few stories years later.

ACTION COMICS No. 127

Above left: *Cover art, Al Plastino, December 1948.*

ACTION COMICS No. 130

Above right: *Cover art, Al Plastino, March 1949.* By the end of the 1940s, real-life celebrities had begun to show up in DC comics on occasion, but a guest appearance with Superman was a singular honor. Actress Ann Blyth's role in *Action Comics* No. 130 promoted her part in the film *Mr. Peabody and the Mermaid.* Game show host and creator Ralph Edwards met the Man of Steel twice, once in 1948 when Superman appears on *Truth or Consequences* and again in 1959's *Superman's Girl Friend, Lois Lane* No. 9, when the girl reporter is the subject of his later program *This Is Your Life.*

THE ADVENTURES OF SUPERMAN

Opposite: *Cover art, Joe Shuster, 1942. The Adventures of Superman* radio writer George Lowther penned the first prose novelization of Superman, with illustrations by the Shuster studio. Lowther used the space to explore themes other media wouldn't get to for years—from life on Krypton and in Smallville, to what it's like to discover you have super-powers as a young man.

The ADVENTURES of SUPERMAN

Superman's adventures, as told in this book, are completely new and have never before appeared anywhere.

By GEORGE LOWTHER

Based on the famous character created by
JOE SHUSTER and JERRY SIEGEL

THE SILVER AGE
1956–1970

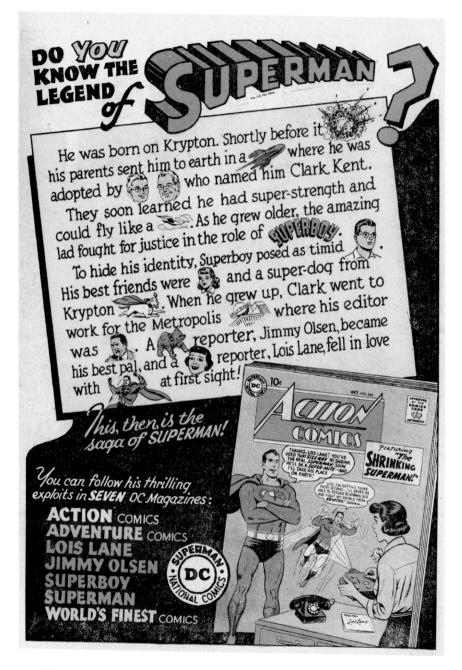

ACTION COMICS No. 357

Previous spread: *Cover art, Curt Swan and George Klein, December 1967.*

SUPERMAN HOUSE AD

Opposite: *Lettering, Ira Schnapp, October 1958.*

ACTION COMICS No. 309

Above: *Cover art, Curt Swan and Sheldon Moldoff, February 1964.*

ACTION COMICS No. 241

Below: *Interior, "The Super-Key to Fort Superman"; script, Jerry Coleman; pencils, Wayne Boring; inks, Stan Kaye. June 1958.* Unlike the Caped Crusader's trophy-laden Batcave, the Fortress of Solitude was more personalized, with elaborate tributes erected to the loved ones he'd lost and the friends he still cherished.

ACTION COMICS No. 241

Opposite: *Cover art, Curt Swan and Stan Kaye, June 1958.*

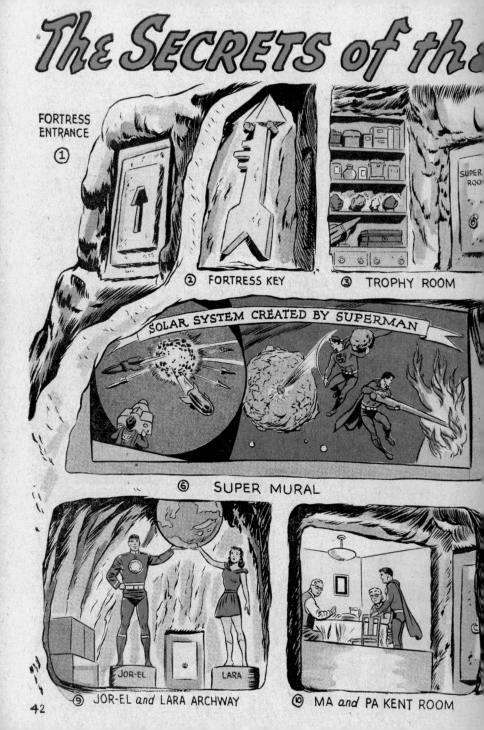

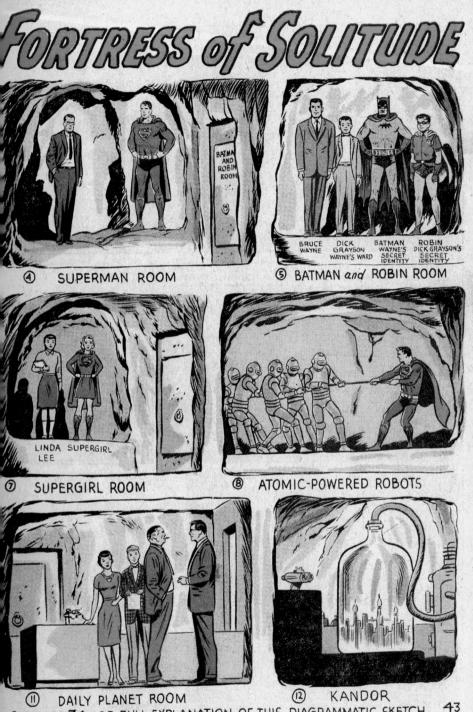

FORTRESS of SOLITUDE

④ SUPERMAN ROOM

⑤ BATMAN and ROBIN ROOM

BRUCE
WAYNE

DICK
GRAYSON
WAYNE'S WARD

BATMAN
WAYNE'S
SECRET
IDENTITY

ROBIN
DICK GRAYSON'S
SECRET
IDENTITY

⑦ SUPERGIRL ROOM

LINDA SUPERGIRL
LEE

⑧ ATOMIC-POWERED ROBOTS

⑪ DAILY PLANET ROOM

⑫ KANDOR

SEE PAGE 74 FOR FULL EXPLANATION OF THIS DIAGRAMMATIC SKETCH. 43

GIANT SUPERMAN ANNUAL No. 3

Previous spread: *Interior, "The Secrets of the Fortress of Solitude"; script, unknown; pencils, Curt Swan; inks, Stan Kaye. Summer 1961.*

ADVENTURE COMICS No. 247

Above: *Cover art, Curt Swan and Stan Kaye, April 1958.*

ACTION COMICS No. 252

Opposite: *Cover art, Curt Swan and Al Plastino, May 1959.*

THE SU

BIZARRO
#1

RMAN FAMILY

SUPERMAN ANNUAL No. 6

Previous spread: *Superman Family pinup, back cover art,
Curt Swan, John Forte (Legionnaires only), and George Klein.
Clockwise, starting from center left, Jonathan and Martha Kent,
Krypto, Streaky, Comet, Mr. Mxyzptlk, Sun Boy, Cosmic Boy,
Lightning Lad, Saturn Girl, and Chameleon Boy of Legion of
Super Heroes, Jor-El and Lara, Lori Lemaris, Bizarro, Professor
Potter, Supergirl and Superman, Lana Lang, Lois Lane, Perry
White, Lucy Lane, Jimmy Olsen, and Beppo. Winter 1962–1963.*

SUPERMAN BALLOON

Opposite: *Photograph, Goodyear Tire and Rubber Company in
Akron, Ohio, ca. 1966.* Built by the Aviation Products Division
of the Goodyear Company, the second Superman balloon to
appear in the Macy's Thanksgiving Day parade made a test
flight in Ohio before traveling to New York City. This balloon
flew in five parades.

SUPERMAN TOOTSIE ROLL AD

Below: *Promotional display, ca. 1961.* Superman has served
as a spokesman for many foods over the years, enough to
form several balanced meals, including desserts. This 1960s
cardboard advertising sign for Tootsie Roll ice cream bars
was designed to sit atop a comic rack and is one of very few
to survive from that era. Similar items have sold on the
collectors market for several thousand dollars.

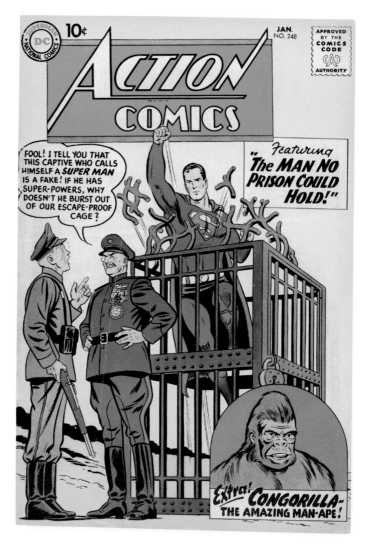

ACTION COMICS No. 248

Above: *Cover art, Curt Swan and Stan Kaye, January 1959.*
Along with Congorilla, editor Mort Weisinger also introduced
recurring simians with human attributes such as Titano and
Beppo the Super-Monkey.

SUPERMAN No. 138

Opposite: *Cover art, Curt Swan and Stan Kaye, July 1960.*

SUPERMAN PSA

Opposite: *Interior, "Lend a Friendly Hand!" from* The Brave and the Bold *No. 31; script, Jack Schiff; pencils, Curt Swan; inks, Stan Kaye. December 1960–January 1961.* In cooperation with several social welfare agencies, editor Jack Schiff routinely prepared public service ads such as this one for all the DC titles, beginning in 1949 and continuing through the mid-1960s. Often inspirational, occasionally preachy, they nonetheless helped cement DC's deserved reputation as a socially responsible publisher.

SUPERMAN'S BUDDY

Above: *Art, Win Mortimer, 1954.*

ACTION COMICS No. 368

Above: *Cover art, Carmine Infantino, October 1968.* The tone of
the stories shifted with the changing culture, but art director
Infantino's effect on the covers was even more visible.

SUPERMAN No. 201

Opposite: *Original cover art, Curt Swan and George Klein,
November 1967.* If Metropolis mirrored the real world, by the
summer of 1967 it wasn't mad scientists in the streets, but
race riots. DC's editors weren't ready to let that much reality
into the comics, but you can see by the slump in Superman's
shoulders of steel that the responsibility was starting to
weigh on him. Being a hero wasn't as easy anymore.

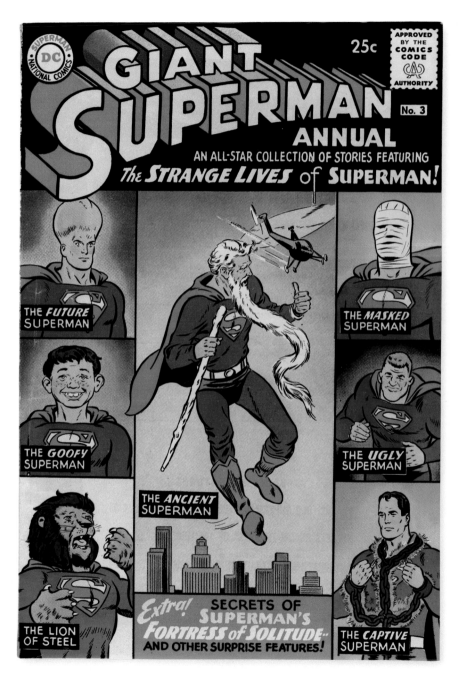

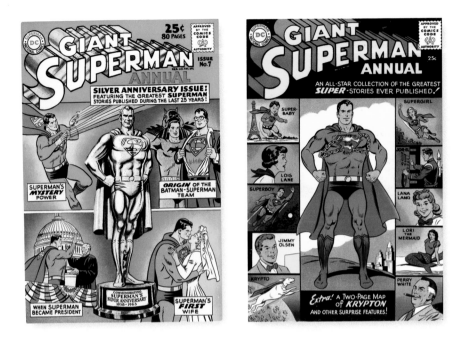

GIANT SUPERMAN ANNUAL No. 3

Opposite: *Cover art, Curt Swan and Stan Kaye, summer 1961.*
Every summer (and every winter — the "Annuals" were in
such demand as to throw the meaning of the word "annual"
out the door), a new Giant Superman would appear on newsstands to much anticipation. These 80-page, squarebound
editions carried more than three times the amount of story
and art as a regular comic, and the fact that they were made
up almost exclusively of previously published material didn't
dull the excitement for most readers.

SUPERMAN ANNUAL No. 7

Above left: *Cover art, Curt Swan and George Klein,
summer 1963.*

SUPERMAN ANNUAL No. 1

Above right: *Cover art, Curt Swan and Stan Kaye, 1960.* If Kurt
Schaffenberger was the definitive Lois Lane artist, Curt Swan
was surely the illustrator who most exemplified Superman
himself, setting the benchmark for generations to come.

ADVENTURE COMICS No. 368

Above: *Cover art, Neal Adams, May 1968.* Most Super Hero
teams could count their female members on one finger,
but the Legion of Super Heroes overflowed with girl power,
boasting nine women to its 15 men in 1968.

SUPERMAN No. 180

Opposite: *Cover art, Curt Swan and George Klein, October 1965.*
In Curt Swan's hands, Superman possessed a degree of vulnerability unseen with previous artists. Readers could clearly
see when he experienced happiness or felt sorrow.

ADVENTURE COMICS No. 346

Below: *Interior, "One of Us Is a Traitor"; script and layout,
Jim Shooter; pencils and inks, Sheldon Moldoff. July 1966.*

ADVENTURE COMICS No. 333

Opposite: *Cover art, Curt Swan and George Klein, June 1965.*
The notion of heroes who didn't always see eye to eye was still
a novelty at 1960s DC but would gradually become mainstream.

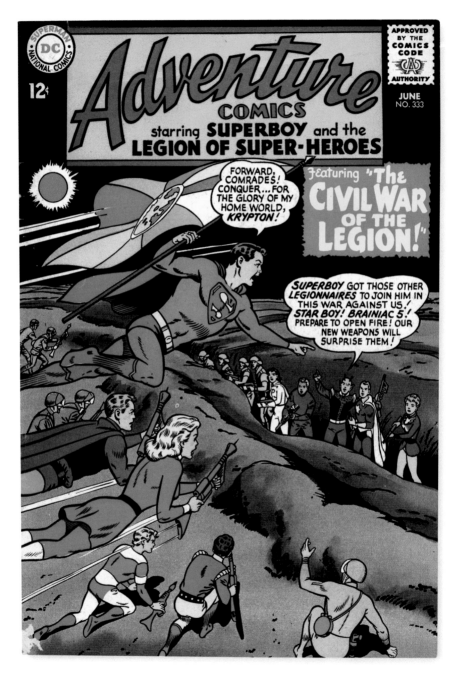

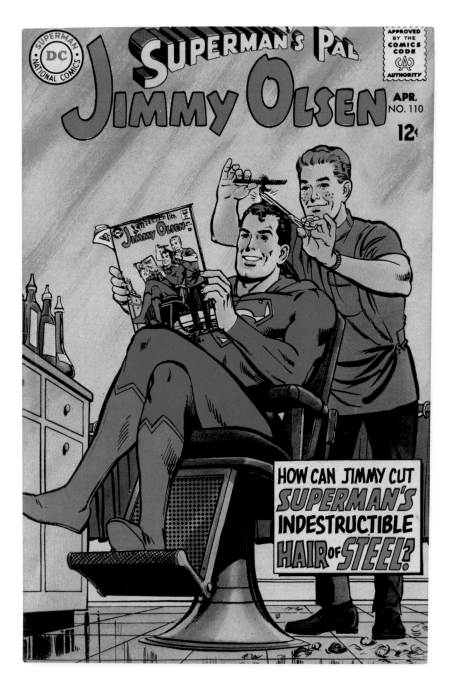

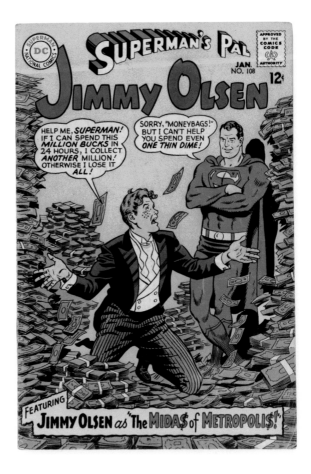

SUPERMAN'S PAL, JIMMY OLSEN No. 110

Opposite: *Cover art, Curt Swan and Neal Adams, April 1968.*
This barber-shop scene is decidedly old-fashioned, not only
in its charming concept but in its use of a 1940s-style "infinity cover," in which characters hold the very comic they're
appearing in as the image shrinks to infinity.

SUPERMAN'S PAL, JIMMY OLSEN No. 108

Above: *Cover art, Curt Swan and George Klein, January 1968.*
For a "pal," Superman could often seem surprisingly unsym-
pathetic to Jimmy, but cover teases and story hooks like this
helped sell the title for years. In this scenario, the red-haired
reporter missed spending a million by a single coin — which
he failed to put in a parking meter.

SUPERMAN'S PAL, JIMMY OLSEN No. 37

Above: *Cover art, Curt Swan and Stan Kaye, June 1959.* More reasonable people would think twice before belting back something labeled "elastic serum," but then again, most people never got to turn invisible, belch flame breath, or catch a fly ball from behind home plate, so who's to judge? See if you can guess which of these was not a transformation Jimmy ever had to endure: (a) human porcupine, (b) six-armed cub reporter, (c) impossibly fat boy, (d) werewolf, (e) king of the giant ants, (f) responsible journalist.

SUPERMAN'S PAL, JIMMY OLSEN No. 53

Opposite: *Cover art, Curt Swan and Stan Kaye, June 1961.* "I used to joke with Weisinger. I said, 'Good God! Here you have this catastrophe. The city is leveled and Superman rebuilds the city.... Think of the thousands of men that were out out of work because of this idiot rebuilding the city!' We laughed about it, but he saw the injustice...the whole concept was ridiculous." —Curt Swan

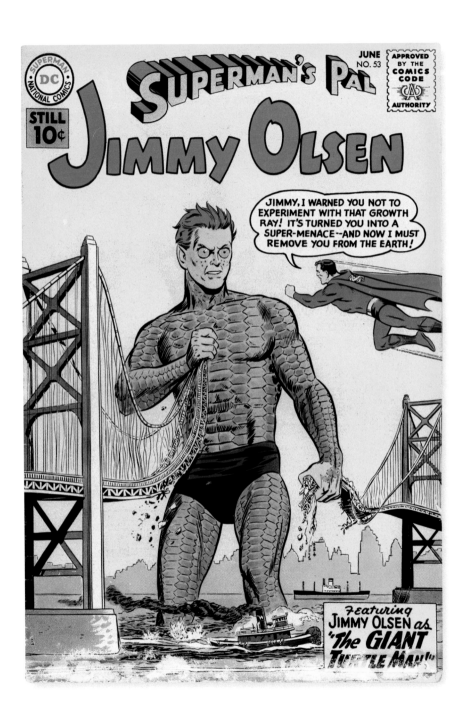

SUPERBOY No. 160

Opposite: *Cover art, Neal Adams, October 1969.* Superboy's soul-searching and questioning of his behavior reflected a society with increasing shades of gray.

SUPERBOY No. 159 HOUSE AD

Below: *Cover art, Neal Adams; lettering, Gaspar Saladino. September 1969.* In 1969, Superboy — "the adventures of Superman when he was a teen" — swerved radically from the complacent Superhouse style once writer Frank Robbins came aboard. Robbins, a veteran of newspaper adventure strips, admitted he'd never read DC comics. His unfamiliarity with the material could have backfired terribly; instead, it worked wonders as he broke rules he didn't know he was breaking. Overnight, the comic was reinvented with realistic teen angst, natural dialogue, and a sex appeal that was only aided by the inks of "good girl" artist Wally Wood.

ACTION COMICS No. 285

Above: *Cover art, Curt Swan and George Klein, February 1962.*
After three years of training as Superman's "secret weapon,"
Supergirl was introduced to the world in the culmination of
a multi-part story that, unlike Superman, allowed the Girl
of Steel to evolve beyond a set status quo.

ACTION COMICS No. 289

Opposite: *Cover art, Curt Swan and George Klein, June 1962.*
Lois Lane had her share of rivals for Superman's affections,
most of them sharing her "L. L." initials. One was Luma Lynai,
the Superwoman from the distant planet Staryl, who would
gladly have taken Superman's hand in marriage had the two
of them not learned — in the nick of time and to their hor-
ror — that Earth's yellow sun was deadly to her.

ACTION COMICS No. 360

Below: *Cover art, Curt Swan and Stan Kaye, March – April 1968.*
This "annual" marks the first time DC collected a serialized story
in a single issue...a prototype for many modern graphic novels.

SUPERBOY No. 89

Opposite: *Interior, "Superboy's Big Brother"; script, Robert
Bernstein; pencils and inks, George Papp. June 1961.*

SUPERBOY, No. 89, June, 1961. Published monthly, with the exception of Feb., May, Aug., and Nov., by NATIONAL COMICS PUBLICATIONS, INC., 2nd and Dickey Sts., SPARTA, ILL. Editorial, Executive offices and Subscriptions, 575 LEXINGTON AVENUE, NEW YORK 22, N. Y. Mort Weisinger, Editor. SECOND CLASS POSTAGE PAID AT SPARTA, ILL. under the act of March 3, 1879. Yearly subscription in the U. S., $1.00 including postage. Foreign, $2.00 in American funds. For advertising rates address Richard A. Feldon & Co., 205 East 42nd St., New York 17, N. Y. © 1961 by Superman, Inc. All rights reserved under International and Pan-American Copyright Conventions. Except for those who have authorized use of their names, the stories, characters and incidents mentioned in this periodical are entirely imaginary and fictitious, and no identification with actual persons, living or dead, is intended or should be inferred. Printed in U.S.A.

I FANTASTICI 3 SUPERMEN

Above left: *Movie poster, Italy, artist unknown, 1967.* Super-mania manifested in Italy in the form of a popular movie series revolving around an FBI agent and two partners. Equipped with bulletproof costumes and other accessories, the Three Supermen fought evil through 1986.

SUPERMAN EL INVENCIBLE

Above right: *Movie poster, 1968.* With the antihero in ascendance during the late 1960s, Italy's wrestler-turned-crimefighter Superargo (played by Giovanni Cianfriglia) was featured in two films wherein the body count he left in his wake made him as bad as the villains he fought.

SUPERMANN IN GERMANY

Opposite: *Photograph, Superman standee, 1966.* After a failed 1953 launch, translated Superman comics from licensed publisher Ehapa made a smash in Germany in 1966. When demand outstripped supply in the early 1980s, DC even produced Superman stories exclusively for the German market.

THE BRONZE AGE
1970–1984

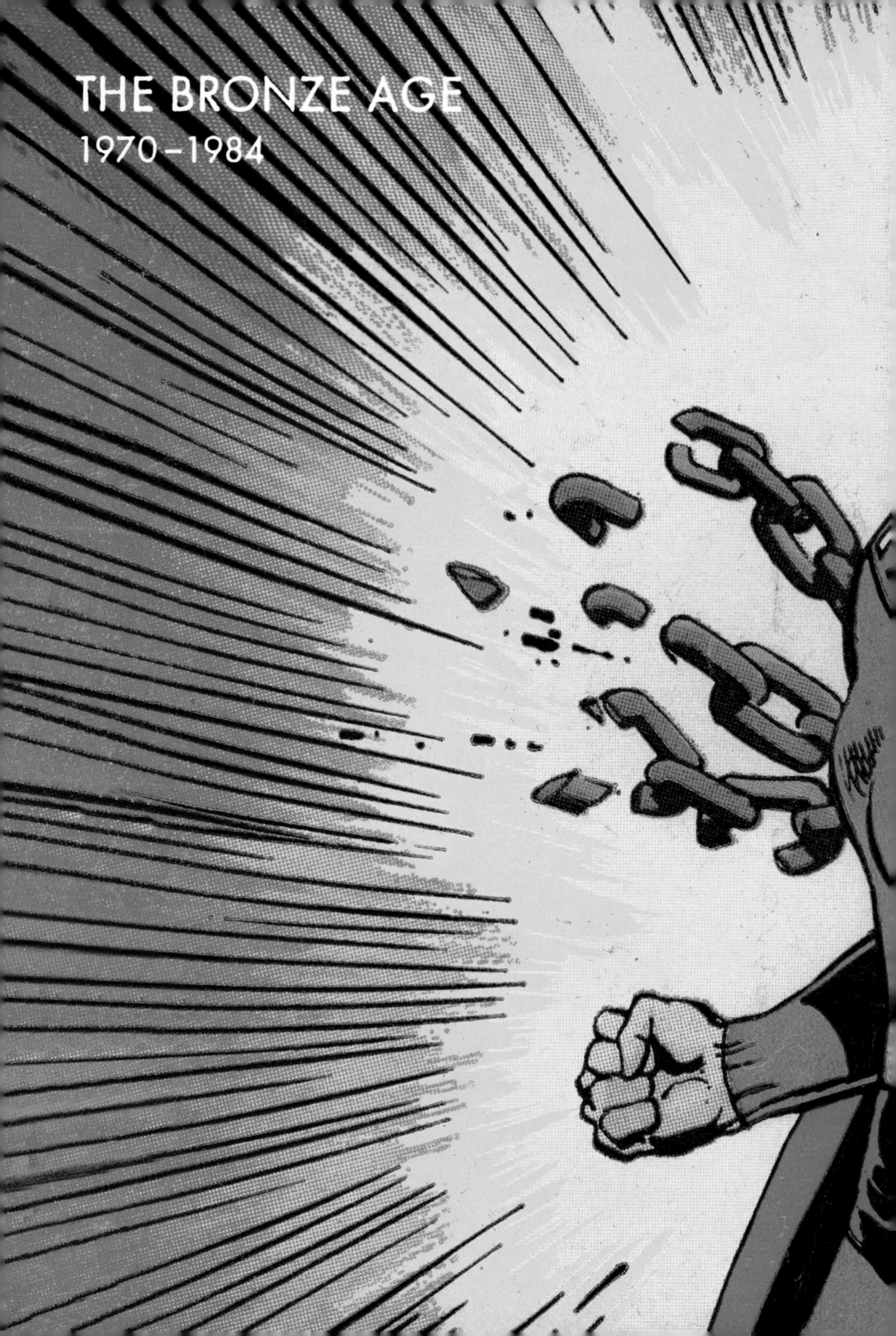

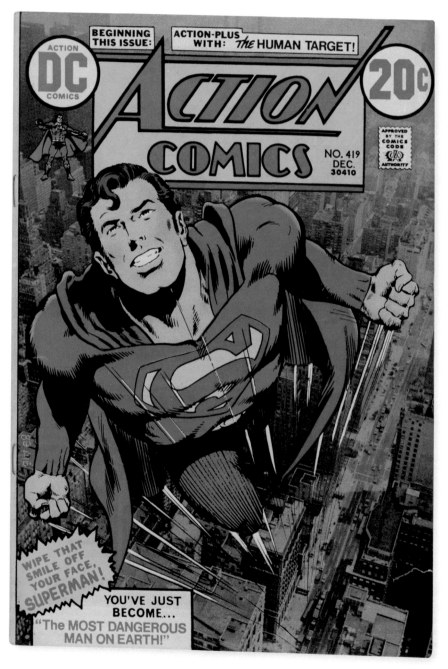

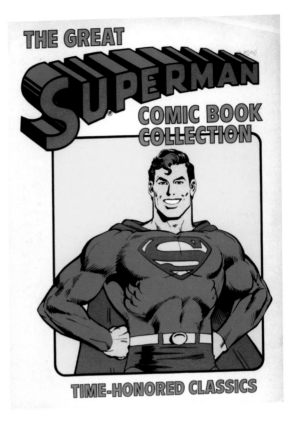

SUPERMAN No. 233

Previous spread: *Cover art, Neal Adams, January 1971.*
Reflecting DC's growing awareness of a fan market that prized
Number Ones, this *Superman* reboot tried to create a first
(issue) impression with its trade dress, while preserving the
series numbering.

ACTION COMICS No. 419

Opposite: *Cover art, Neal Adams, Murphy Anderson, and Jack
Adler, December 1972.*

THE GREAT SUPERMAN COMIC BOOK
COLLECTION

Above: *Cover art, José Luis García-López and Dick Giordano,
1981.* Developed as a premium and later distributed to retail-
ers, *The Great Superman Comic Book Collection* was the first
trade paperback published directly by DC.

SHOWTIME—THE RETURN OF SUPERMAN

Below: *Cover art,* The Press, *José Luis García-López and Dick Giordano, Thursday, November 30, 1978.*

MACY'S THANKSGIVING DAY PARADE

Opposite: *Photograph, Superman balloon on Thanksgiving, New York City, ca. 1982.* The largest Macy's balloon ever— measuring 107 feet—was a Superman first seen in 1980. To get the face correct, Sol Harrison and Dick Giordano went to the hangar where it was built, and painted with the construction crew. It differed from the two previous versions in that the hands were separate chambers, one of which deflated in 1980. The following year, one hand fell off and had to be carried to parade's end. There were no mishaps in the third year, but a balloon this size was apparently considered too unwieldy and did not make a fourth appearance.

The return of Superman

SUPERMAN'S PAL, JIMMY OLSEN No. 137

Above: *Cover art, Jack Kirby and Neal Adams, April 1971.* "There was something about the interconnectedness of those Fourth World titles, which hit me at a time when I was just starting to think about questions of narrative, storytelling, and world-making. The way that Kirby came into the DC world that I was already familiar with and reoriented the entire thing with his own vision of Super Hero myth. And did it in a way that has turned out to be very lasting…" — Michael Chabon

SUPERMAN'S PAL JIMMY OLSEN No. 146

Opposite: *Original cover art, Jack Kirby and Mike Royer, February 1972.*

SUPERMAN'S PAL, JIMMY OLSEN No. 137

Previous spread: *Interior, "The Four-Armed Terror"; script, pencils, and photo collage, Jack Kirby; inks, Vince Colletta. April 1971.* Readers accustomed to DC's more traditional and sedate storytelling techniques must have found Kirby's arrival — especially on Jimmy Olsen — eye popping. The use of photo collage was just one of many innovations "The King of the Comics" brought with him.

SUPER HEALTHY COOKBOOK

Above: *Book cover and interior, 1981.* The original cover for a DC-themed cookbook was rejected as too abstract. "It was a sunny yellow wraparound with fruits in Super Hero regalia on the front," Jenette Kahn recalled. "On the back, all that was left of the fruit were the cores, the Super Hero costumes scattered on the ground."

FULL TILT

Opposite: *Superman pinball machine, Atari, 1979.*

THE DAILY PLANET

Above: *Movie prop, facsimile newspaper*, Superman III, *1983*.
The movie's Daily Planet as shown here bore no physical
resemblance to the real-life paper "playing" it: many scenes
were filmed in front of the offices and in the lobby of the tabloid
New York Daily News.

SUPERMAN THE MOVIE

Opposite: *Poster, featuring Christopher Reeve as Superman,*
Warner Bros. Pictures, *1978*. In 1978, there had never been
anything like the first, smash-hit *Superman* film, with its
state-of-the-art effects and all-star cast supporting newcomer
Reeve. Most happily for comics fans, it restored Superman's
popularity and led to long-deferred public recognition of
Siegel and Shuster as the character's creators.

SPECIAL EFFECTS

Opposite: *Photograph, Christopher Reeve and director Richard Donner on the set of* Superman II, *1978.* Here, Reeve is seen on the boom used in special effects designer Zoltan Perisic's "Zoptic" process. It created the never-before-seen effect of Superman flying into the camera. Reeve's physique was at first less than heroic, but he bulked up thanks to a training regimen with stuntman David (Darth Vader) Prowse.

SUPERMAN II

Below: *Film still,* Superman II, *1980. Superman II's* success clinched it: Adult audiences really were ready to take a Super Hero, previously thought to be strictly kids' stuff, as seriously as they did any Clint Eastwood character.

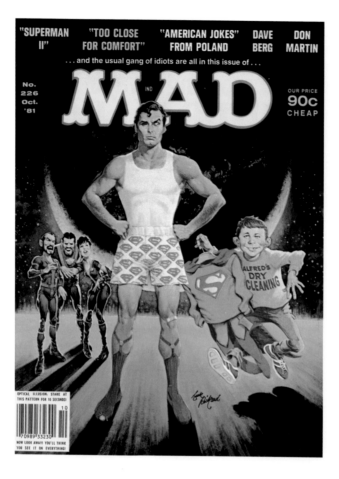

MAD No. 226

Above: *Cover art, Jack Rickard, October 1981.* In its first parody of the Man of Steel in 1953, Mad dubbed him Superduperman. Mort Drucker illustrated take-offs of the first three films in the late 1970s and early 1980s, by which time he'd been rechristened Stuporman.

NEARLY EXPOSED

Opposite: *Film still, Reeve and Aaron Smolinski by the photo booth, Superman III, 1983.* To moviegoers, this little boy was just another uncredited extra, but to the producers of the Superman series, he was an old colleague who had been with them from the beginning. Five years earlier, Aaron Smolinski had played Baby Kal-El in the first film.

film produkcji
angielskiej

reż: Richard Lester

w rolach głównych:
Christopher Reeve
Richard Pryor
Jackie Cooper

prod: Devomead
for
Cantharus
Productions
1983

SUPERMAN III

SUPERMAN IN JAPAN

Opposite: *Poster, artist unknown, 1981.* International audiences
sometimes saw more differences in the U.S. Superman films
than just the translated dialogue. Europe's home video version
of Supergirl actually ran twenty minutes longer than the U.S.
incarnation, and was available on Japanese laserdisc.

POLISH SUPERMAN III POSTER

Above: *Art, Waldemar Swierzy, 1983. Superman III* tried to broaden
the film's appeal by co-starring comedian Richard Pryor, but an
entirely different tactic was taken in this Polish movie poster.

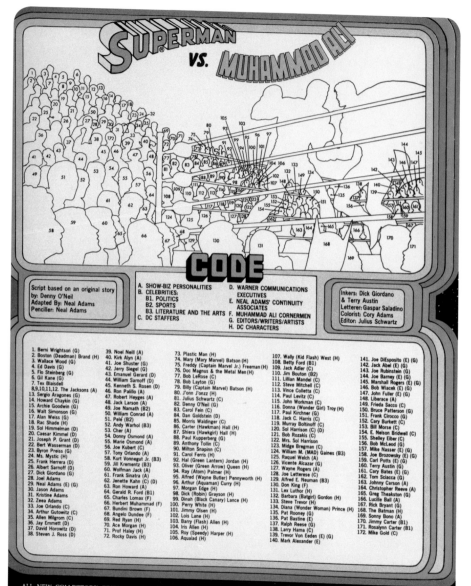

CODE

Script based on an original story
by: Denny O'Neil
Adapted By: Neal Adams
Penciller: Neal Adams

A. SHOW-BIZ PERSONALITIES
B. CELEBRITIES:
  B1. POLITICS
  B2. SPORTS
  B3. LITERATURE AND THE ARTS
C. DC STAFFERS

D. WARNER COMMUNICATIONS EXECUTIVES
E. NEAL ADAMS' CONTINUITY ASSOCIATES
F. MUHAMMAD ALI CORNERMEN
G. EDITORS/WRITERS/ARTISTS
H. DC CHARACTERS

Inkers: Dick Giordano
& Terry Austin
Letterer: Gaspar Saladino
Colorist: Cory Adams
Editor: Julius Schwartz

1. Berni Wrightson (G)
2. Boston (Deadman) Brand (H)
3. Wallace Wood (G)
4. Ed Davis (G)
5. Flo Steinberg (G)
6. Gil Kane (G)
7. Tex Blaisdell (G)
8,9,10,11,12. The Jacksons (A)
13. Sergio Aragones (G)
14. Howard Chaykin (G)
15. Archie Goodwin (G)
16. Walt Simonson (G)
17. Alan Weiss (G)
18. Rac Shade (H)
19. Sol Himmelman (D)
20. Caesar Kimmel (D)
21. Joseph P. Grant (D)
22. Bert Wasserman (D)
23. Byron Preiss (G)
24. Ms. Mystic (H)
25. Frank Herrera (D)
26. Albert Sarnoff (D)
27. Dick Giordano (G)
28. Joel Adams
29. Neal Adams (E) (G)
30. Jason Adams
31. Kristine Adams
32. Zeea Adams
33. Joe Orlando (G)
34. Arthur Gutowitz (C)
35. Allen Milgrom (C)
36. Jay Emmett (D)
37. David Horowitz (D)
38. Steven J. Ross (D)

39. Noel Neill (A)
40. Kirk Alyn (A)
41. Joe Shuster (G)
42. Jerry Siegel (G)
43. Emanuel Gerard (D)
44. William Sarnoff (D)
45. Kenneth S. Rosen (D)
46. Ron Palillo (A)
47. Robert Heyges (A)
48. Jack Larson (A)
49. Joe Namath (B2)
50. William Conrad (A)
51. Pelé (B2)
52. Andy Warhol (B3)
53. Cher (A)
54. Donny Osmond (A)
55. Marie Osmond (A)
56. Joe Kubert (G)
57. Tony Orlando (A)
58. Kurt Vonnegut Jr. (B3)
59. Jill Krementz (B3)
60. Wolfman Jack (A)
61. Frank Sinatra (A)
62. Jenette Kahn (C) (D)
63. Ron Howard (A)
64. Gerald R. Ford (B1)
65. Charles Lomax (F)
66. Herbert Muhammad (F)
67. Bundini Brown (F)
68. Angelo Dundee (F)
69. Red Ryan (H)
70. Ace Morgan (H)
71. Prof Haley (H)
72. Rocky Davis (H)

73. Plastic Man (H)
74. Mary (Mary Marvel) Batson (H)
75. Freddy (Captain Marvel Jr.) Freeman (H)
76. Doc Magnus & the Metal Men (H)
77. Bob LeRose (C)
78. Bob Layton (G)
79. Billy (Captain Marvel) Batson (H)
80. J'onn J'onzz (H)
81. Julius Schwartz (C)
82. Denny O'Neil (G)
83. Carol Fein (C)
84. Dan Goldstein (D)
85. Morris Waldinger (C)
86. Carter (Hawkman) Hall (H)
87. Shiera (Hawkgirl) Hall (H)
88. Paul Kupperberg (G)
89. Anthony Tollin (C)
90. Milton Snapinn (C)
91. Carol Ferris (H)
92. Hal (Green Lantern) Jordan (H)
93. Oliver (Green Arrow) Queen (H)
94. Ray (Atom) Palmer (H)
95. Alfred (Wayne Butler) Pennyworth (H)
96. Arthur (Aquaman) Curry (H)
97. Morgan Edge (H)
98. Dick (Robin) Grayson (H)
99. Dinah (Black Canary) Lance (H)
100. Perry White (H)
101. Jimmy Olsen (H)
102. Lois Lane (H)
103. Barry (Flash) Allen (H)
104. Iris Allen (H)
105. Roy (Speedy) Harper (H)
106. Aqualad (H)

107. Wally (Kid Flash) West (H)
108. Betty Ford (B1)
109. Jack Adler (C)
110. Jim Bouton (B2)
111. Lillian Mandel (C)
112. Steve Mitchell (C)
113. Vince Colletta (C)
114. Paul Levitz (C)
115. John Workman (C)
116. Donna (Wonder Girl) Troy (H)
117. Paul Kirchner (C)
118. Jack C. Harris (C)
119. Murray Boltinoff (C)
120. Sol Harrison (C) (D)
121. Bob Rozakis (C)
122. Mrs. Sol Harrison
123. Midge Bregman (C)
124. William M. (MAD) Gaines (B3)
125. Raquel Welch (A)
126. Vicente Alcazar (G)
127. Wayne Rogers (A)
128. Joe Letterese (C)
129. Alfred E. Neuman (B3)
130. Don King (F)
131. Lex Luthor (H)
132. Barbara (Batgirl) Gordon (H)
133. Steve Trevor (H)
134. Diana (Wonder Woman) Prince (H)
135. Pat Rooney (G)
136. Pat Bastine (C)
137. Ralph Reese (G)
138. Larry Hama (C)
139. Trevor Von Eeden (E) (G)
140. Mark Alexander (E)

141. Joe DiEsposito (E) (G)
142. Jack Abel (E) (G)
143. Joe Rubinstein (G)
144. Joe Barney (E) (G)
145. Marshall Rogers (E) (G)
146. Bob Wiacek (E) (G)
147. John Fuller (E) (G)
148. Liberace (A)
149. Frieda Sacco (C)
150. Bruce Patterson (G)
151. Frank Cirocco (G)
152. Cary Burkett (C)
153. Bill Morse (C)
154. E. Nelson Bridwell (C)
155. Shelley Eiber (C)
156. Bob McLeod (G)
157. Mike Nasser (E) (G)
158. Joe Brozowsky (E) (G)
159. Carl Potts (E) (G)
160. Terry Austin (G)
161. Cary Bates (E) (G)
162. Tom Sciacca (G)
163. Johnny Carson (A)
164. Christopher Reeve (A)
165. Greg Theakston (G)
166. Lucille Ball (A)
167. Rick Bryant (G)
168. The Batman (H)
169. Sonny Bono (A)
170. Jimmy Carter (B1)
171. Rosalynn Carter (B1)
172. Mike Gold (C)

ALL NEW COLLECTORS' EDITION, Vol. 7, No. C-56, 1978. Published quarterly by DC COMICS INC., 75 Rockefeller Plaza, New York, N.Y. 10019. Copyright © 1978 by DC Comics Inc. All Rights Reserved. The stories, and incidents mentioned in this magazine are entirely fictional. Printed in U.S.A.

Jenette Kahn, Publisher
Joe Orlando, Managing Editor
Julius Schwartz, Editor
E. Nelson Bridwell, Associate Editor
Jack Adler, Vice-Pres. Production
Vince Colletta, Art Director
Paul Levitz, Editorial Coordinator

Sol Harrison, President
Arthur Gutowitz, Treasurer

SUPERMAN VS. MUHAMMAD ALI

Previous spread: *Cover art, Neal Adams, 1978.* Another historic tabloid pitting the Man of Steel against an unlikely opponent, this cover was famous for its ringside cameos by many celebrities, including Michael Jackson, the Beatles, and two American presidents.

SUPERMAN VS. MUHAMMAD ALI KEY

Opposite: *Interior, key to celebrities and DC characters in the audience on Neal Adams's wraparound cover, 1978.* Not all 172 likenesses were nationally known celebrities. Many were comics industry figures known only to fans, who delighted in finding their faces.

THE GREATEST

Above: *Photograph, left to right, Don King, Herbert Muhammad, and Muhammad Ali at a press conference with Sol Harrison, 1977.*

SUPERMAN No. 408

Below: *Cover art, Ed Hannigan and Al Williamson, June 1985*
With tensions running high between the United States and
Soviet Union during the last years of the Cold War, a 1985
story found the Man of Steel haunted by nightmares of a
global nuclear war. Although he considered disarming the
world's nuclear arsenal, Superman ultimately decided that
he couldn't mother hen the human race.

SUPERMAN No. 240

Opposite: *Cover art, Neal Adams, July 1971*. The fickle nature
of public acclaim was a recurring theme during the Superman
stories of the 1960s. That didn't stop in the following decade,
as the Man of Steel learned during the ongoing serial in which
his powers were progressively weakened.

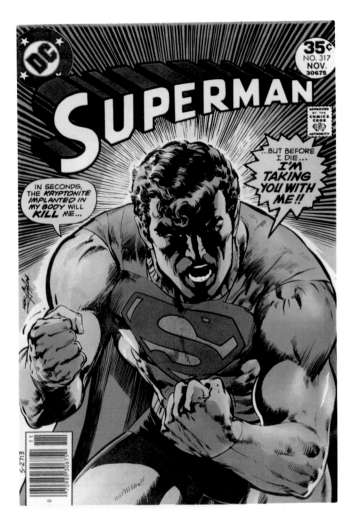

THE PHANTOM ZONE No. 4

Opposite: *Interior, "The Phantom Planet"; script, Steve Gerber; pencils, Gene Colan; inks, Tony DeZuniga. April 1982.* Another artist whose Superman was a rare treat in the day when most Super Heroes were handled by the same, small talent pool was Gene Colan, here joining *Howard the Duck* collaborator Gerber on a memorable miniseries.

SUPERMAN No. 317

Above: *Cover art, Neal Adams, November 1977.*

ACTION COMICS No. 541

Opposite: *Cover art, Gil Kane, March 1983.*

SUPERMAN No. 321

Below: *Cover art, José Luis García-López and Dick Giordano, March 1978.* 1970's less-powerful Superman was abandoned by 1975, and finding suitable challenges for him again became daunting. The occasional solution was turning his own powers — such as super-hearing — against him.

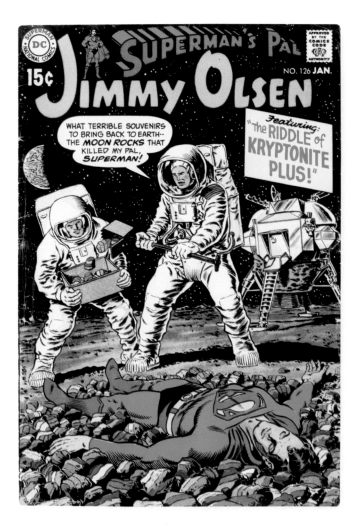

SUPERMAN'S PAL, JIMMY OLSEN No. 126

Above: *Cover art, Curt Swan and Murphy Anderson, January 1970.* Published just months after 1969's first moon landing, Jimmy Olsen imagined a worst case scenario: some of the moon rocks were actually lethal Kryptonite! Naturally, it was all a hoax.

IT'S A KILLER

Opposite: *Cover art*, The Best of DC *No. 36; Ed Hannigan and Dick Giordano, May 1983.*

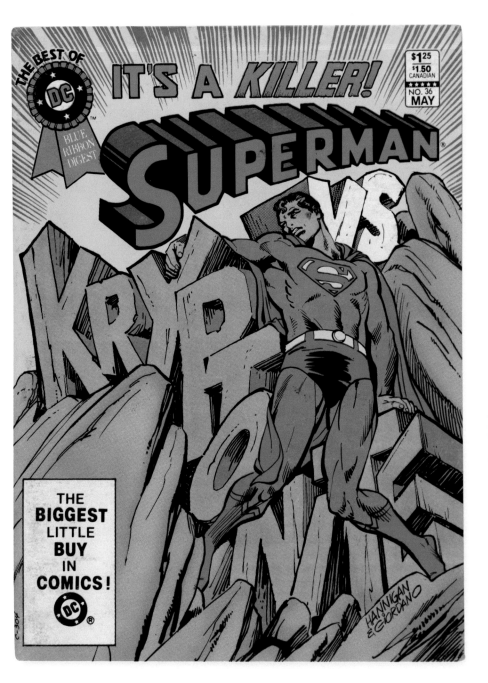

 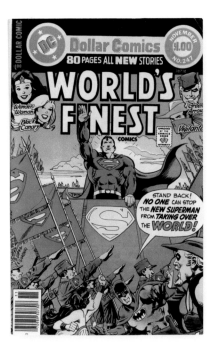

SUPERMAN No. 349

Above left: *Cover art, Ross Andru and Dick Giordano.*
January – February 1977.

WORLD'S FINEST COMICS No. 247

Above right: *Cover art, José Luis García-López and*
Dick Giordano. October – November 1977.

ALL-STAR COMICS No. 64

Opposite: *Cover art, Wally Wood, January – February 1977. All-*
Star's revival is fondly remembered as one of several DC titles
of the 1970s that published the last mainstream comics work
of the legendary Wallace Wood, of EC fame, who died in 1981.
This issue was particularly noteworthy because Wood (and
his assistants) illustrated it in its entirety, rather than working
over others' layouts, and the story reflected Wood's request to
writer Paul Levitz to include Superman and knights in armor.

ACTION COMICS No. 445

Opposite: *Cover art, Nick Cardy, March 1975.*

SUPERMAN No. 276

Above left: *Cover art, Nick Cardy, June 1974.* Fans who knew how Superman and Shazam! had metaphorically battled, when DC and Fawcett fought over copyright infringement, often fantasized about an "actual" battle between the two heroes. Soon after *Shazam!* hit the stands, DC teased readers with such a battle by introducing Captain Thunder, an Earth-One version of the Big Red Cheese.

SUPERMAN No. 242

Above right: *Cover art, Neal Adams, September 1971.*

ACTION COMICS No. 388

Above: *Cover art, Curt Swan and Murphy Anderson, May 1970.*
A deranged Superman cover overflowed with deliberate errors
that were obvious to devoted fans. Among those details was
the Man of Steel wearing Clark Kent's glasses, Perry White
smoking a pipe rather than his trademark cigar, Brainiac
wearing Mr. Mxyzptlk's costume and Krypto the Superdog
sporting the colors of Streaky the Supercat.

SUPERMAN No. 270

Opposite: *Interior, "I Can't Go Home Again": script, Elliot S!*
Maggin; pencils and inks, Murphy Anderson. December 1973.
In this period, action-packed *Superman* lead stories were
paired with lighter or more introspective shorts about the
character's non-super dimensions. This was an early entry
in a series that ran for many years.

DC SPECIAL SERIES No. 26

Below: *Interior, "Fortress of Fear"; script, Roy Thomas; pencils, Ross Andru; inks, Romeo Tanghal. Summer 1981.* Among Roy Thomas's first assignments for DC was a research-heavy project that drew on old Superman stories to create a history of the Fortress of Solitude. The tabloid-sized tie-in to the *Superman II* film included a through-line in which the Man of Steel had to stop a dire chain of events that would trigger an atomic reaction within the Fortress that would destroy the Earth.

SUPERMAN No. 307

Opposite: *Cover art, Neal Adams, January 1977.*

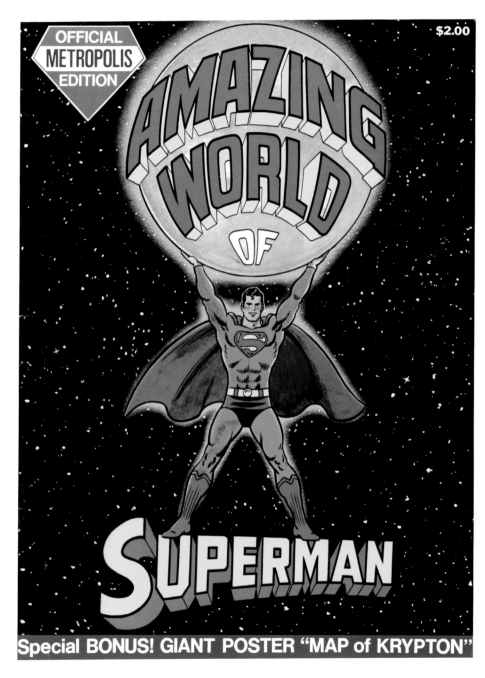

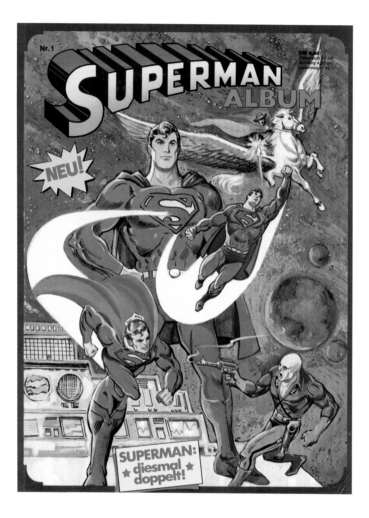

THE AMAZING WORLD OF SUPERMAN, METROPOLIS EDITION

Opposite: *Cover art, Curt Swan and Murphy Anderson, 1973.*
In 1972, Metropolis, Illinois hoped to capitalize on its name
by transforming itself into a destination spot for Superman
fans with a massive theme park and statue. In support of the
project, DC produced a tabloid-sized souvenir edition that
included a definitive retelling of the Man of Steel's origin.

SUPERMAN ALBUM No. 1

Above: *Cover art, Adrian Gonzales and Joe Orlando, 1982.*

AMAZING WORLD OF DC COMICS

Above left: *Cover art, No. 2, Kurt Schaffenberger, September–
October 1974.* Above right: *Cover art, No. 10, Murphy Anderson
and Jack Adler (photo elements), January 1976.* Young staffers
and paid interns dubbed themselves the "Junior Woodchucks"
and were given the opportunity to create DC's own subscrip-
tion-based fanzine … doing everything from writing and
paste-up to stuffing copies in envelopes to mail after they'd
hauled up the printed copies from the loading dock.

LIMITED COLLECTORS' EDITION No. C-38

Opposite: *Cover art, Curt Swan and Bob Oksner,
October–November 1975.*

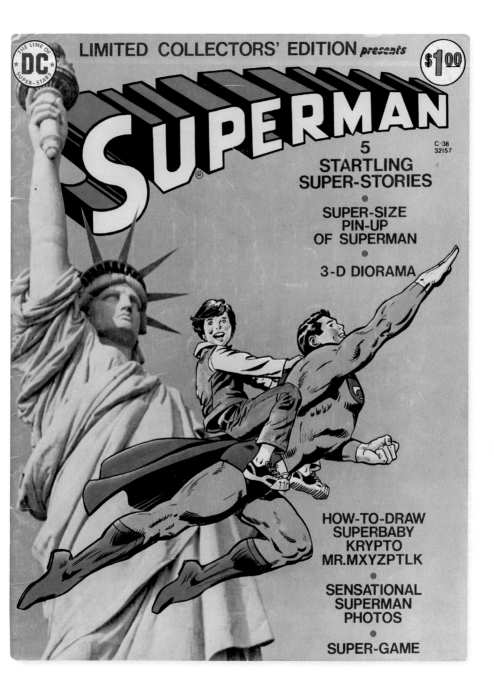

SUPERMAN PIN-UPS

Opposite and above: *Pin-up art by Bill Sienkiewicz, Jim Steranko, and Moebius, October 1984.* It seemed fitting to mark this publishing milestone by appealing to the comics-literate fans' curiosity about how Superman would be interpreted by the medium's masters. In addition to the industry giants seen here, *Superman* No. 400 featured art by Howard Chaykin, *MAD*'s Jack Davis, M. W. Kaluta, Jack Kirby, Frank Miller, Jerry Robinson, Marshall Rogers, Walt Simonson, Leonard Starr, Al Williamson, and Bernie Wrightson, among others.

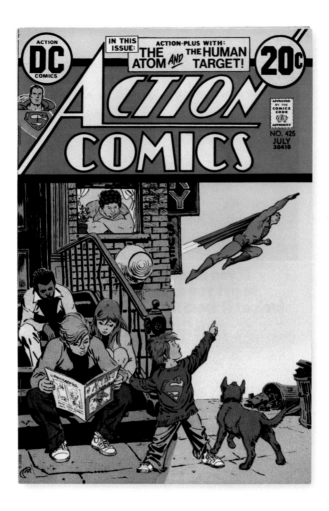

ACTION COMICS No. 425

Above: *Cover art, Nick Cardy, July 1973.*

MAY CO. PRESENTS SUPERMAN

Opposite: *Advertising art, unknown, 1979.* The release of
Superman: The Movie was a licensing bonanza that gener-
ated countless books, toys, and other products. For Michael
Fleisher, whose *Encyclopedia of Comic Book Heroes* had stalled
after editions devoted to Batman and Wonder Woman, it
was an opportunity to get his Superman volume into print,
rebranded as *The Great Superman Book.*

THE NEW ADVENTURES OF SUPERBOY No. 40

Opposite: *Cover art, Howard Bender and Dick Giordano, April 1983.* As hipper teenage heroes like the New Teen Titans stole the spotlight in the 1980s, Superboy struggled to stay relevant with fans. One lengthy subplot followed Clark Kent's high school romance with classmate Lisa Davis, who preferred the bookish teenager to his flashy alter ego.

THE AMAZING WORLD OF SUPERMAN CONCEPT SKETCH

Below: *Proposed theme park art, Neal Adams, ca. 1973.* Since 1972, Metropolis, Illinois, has been a major Midwestern tourist attraction, having proclaimed itself the "Hometown of Superman." DC and private developers proposed that Metropolis could become the site of a Superman theme park, as envisioned in designs it commissioned from Adams.

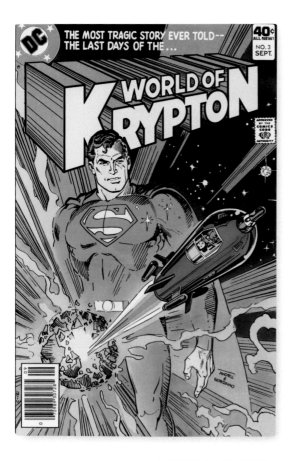

WORLD OF KRYPTON No. 3

Above: *Cover art, Ross Andru and Dick Giordano, September 1979.*

SUPERMAN No. 400

Opposite: *Interior, "The Living Legends of Superman"; script, Elliot S! Maggin; pencils and inks, Frank Miller. October 1984.*
Frank Miller started at DC as an illustrator, but he returned for *Ronin* in control of his projects. *The Dark Knight Returns* was a perfect expression of Miller's noir sensibilities, starring an aging Batman spurred out of retirement by gang violence in later Gotham. Klaus Janson's heavy inks and Lynn Varley's muted colors suited this dark tale, which exemplified the maturation of the superhero. *The Dark Knight* also featured Superman as a well-meaning but naive presidential puppet. In *Superman No. 400*, Miller illustrated Elliot S! Maggin's anniversary salute to the Man of Steel.

THE DARK AGE
1984–1998

BATMAN: THE DARK KNIGHT No. 3

Previous spread: *Interior, "Hunt the Dark Knight"; script and pencils, Frank Miller; inks, Klaus Janson. 1986.*

THE MAN OF STEEL No. 1

Above: *Cover art, John Byrne, 1986.*

CRISIS ON INFINITE EARTHS No. 7

Oppostie: *Cover art, George Pérez, October 1985.* A shattered Superman holds the lifeless body of his cousin Kara Zor-El on one of the most famous — and imitated — comic book covers of all time. Artist George Pérez included a who's who of mourners along the perspective lines radiating from the two central figures. In 2006, fans voted it their favorite DC cover by a wide margin.

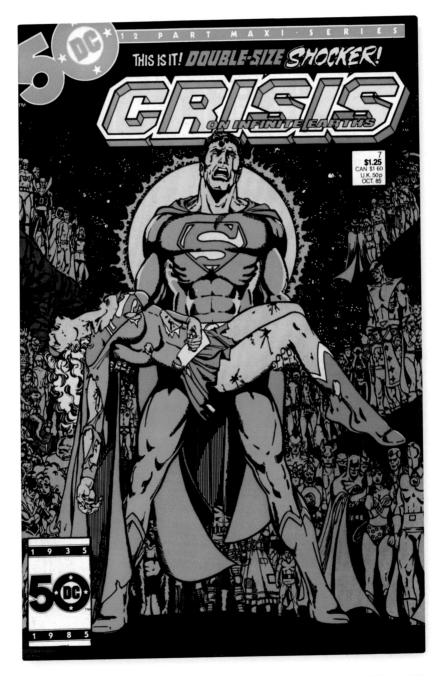

ACTION COMICS No. 583

Below: *Cover art, Ed Hannigan (layout), Curt Swan, and Murphy Anderson, September 1986.*

THE ADVENTURES OF SUPERMAN No. 424

Opposite: *Cover art, Jerry Ordway, January 1987.* Byrne's revamp led to a relaunched *Superman* ongoing title with a new issue No. 1, while the series' original numbering continued in the retitled *Adventures of Superman.* Popular *Teen Titans* and *Crisis* writer Marv Wolfman contributed the initial stories with art by Jerry Ordway.

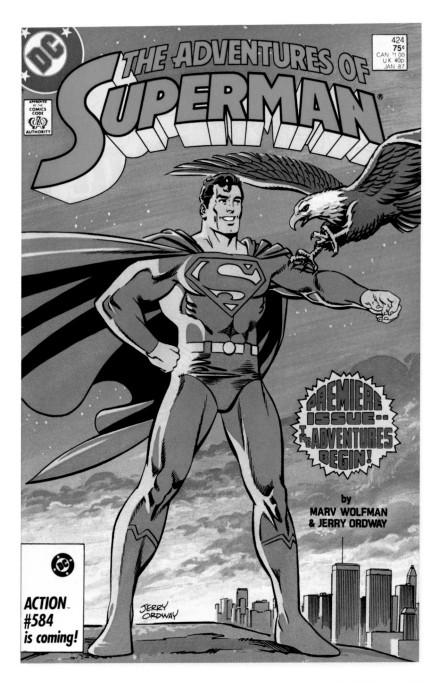

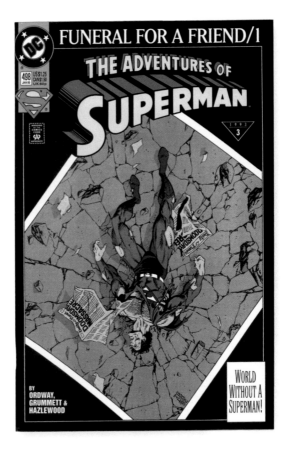

SUPERMAN: THE MAN OF STEEL No. 19

Opposite: *Interior, "Doomsday Is Here"; script, Louise Simonson; pencils, Jon Bogdanove; inks, Dennis Janke. January 1993.*
In a succession of weekly issues, the alien Doomsday emerged from deep under the ground and marched toward Metropolis, with no force on Earth able to halt his progress. To convey the mounting tension, the panels grew larger with each issue. Four panels per page gave way to three and then two, with the increased canvas communicating intensity and immediacy. The final issue of the arc contained a single panel on each page (also known as a splash page) with Lois's anguished reaction to Superman's death appearing as a three-page gatefold.

ADVENTURES OF SUPERMAN No. 498

Above: *Cover art, Tom Grummett and Doug Hazelwood, January 1993.*

SUPERMAN No. 75

Above: *Cover art, Dan Jurgens and Brett Breeding, January 1993.*
The stark image of the Man of Steel's tattered cape graced the
cover of the issue featuring his death at the hands of the unstop-
pable Doomsday. Reflecting an era that saw an increased focus
on comics as collectibles, an alternate "memorial set" version
of the issue featured a tombstone cover inside a black polybag.
Along with the comic book, the package contained stamps, a
poster, a trading card, an obituary from the *Daily Planet*, and
a mourning armband.

SUPERMAN No. 78

Opposite: *Interior poster art, Dan Jurgens and Brett Breeding,
June 1993.*

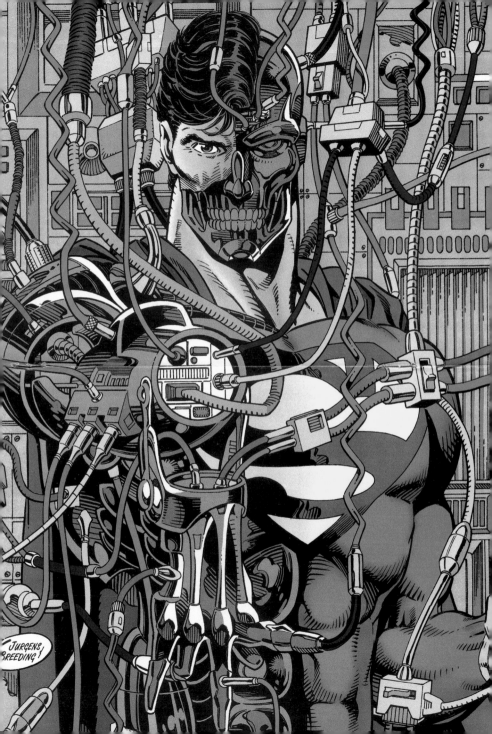

AN EVENING WITH SUPERMAN

Left: *Pencils for unpublished project, Barry Windsor-Smith, 1997.* This oversize art book has entered fan folklore because of the years it has spent in limbo. Windsor-Smith conceived of the project as a lush visual exploration of Metropolis and its characters told through the prism of the first meeting between Superman and Lois Lane.

FOR REFERENCE ONLY
TM © DC COMICS 1997
Superman Costume SC3

SUPERMAN LIVES

Above: *Costume design for unproduced movie, Warner Bros.
Pictures, 1997.* A new Superman movie began to take shape
in the 1990s, with a script by Kevin Smith and *Batman's* Tim
Burton attached as director. Several costume designs were
prepared before the studio shut down the project.

KINGDOM COME No. 2

Opposite: *Interior, "Truth and Justice"; script, Mark Waid;
painted art, Alex Ross, 1996.* The old heroes return in a spec-
tacular splash page from the second issue. Ross and Waid put
considerable thought into creating "20 years later" versions
of familiar faces and employed a combination of costume
changes, new code names, physical transformations, and
next-generation legacy characters. Surrounding Superman,
clockwise from upper right, is Hawkman (now a bird-headed
god), Power Woman, the Flash (no longer able to stop vibrat-
ing), Green Lantern, Wonder Woman, and the Ray.

SUPERMAN: THE MAN OF STEEL No. 121

Previous Spread: *Cover art, Lee Bermejo, February 2002.*

ALL STAR SUPERMAN No. 10

Above: *Interior, "Neverending"; script, Grant Morrison; pencils, Frank Quitely; inks, Jamie Grant. May 2008.*

IT'S A BIRD . . .

Opposite: *Interior, "It's a Bird…"; script, Steven T. Seagle; pencils and inks, Teddy Kristiansen. 2004.* Steven T. Seagle wrote the graphic novel *It's a Bird…* to explore the underpinnings of Superman as a character and a symbol, as well as the autobiographical impact of Huntington's disease on his family. Published by Vertigo, *It's a Bird…* won an Eisner Award for artist Teddy Kristiansen. On this page, Kristiansen and Seagle tackle a discussion of color through a nine-panel grid that spotlights the variations in repeated images.

RED, YELLOW, BLUE

You're as much America as jazz, baseball, or the comic book--

--but you're not red, white and blue.

You're clad in the triad of primary colors: red, yellow, blue--

--the three hues from which all other colors are created.

Is red-yellow-blue some kind of pre-political correctness?

Do you represent men of all colors?

Or is it more mechanical than that? Did Jerry Siegel and Joe Shuster choose red-yellow-blue because of the arcane printing limitations of 1938?

Or was there some chromatic alchemy at work?

A secret spectrum specifically chosen for its symbolic meanings?

Red. The color of war. Mars is the God of War.

The red planet is Mars. Another planet. Alien origin.

Red is a masculine color. The color of life and fire. Energy and aggression are also red, but so are love and passion.

The red heart. Blood red. Blood is the force of life. In Christianity, red is the color of sacrificial blood. Would you die for us?

Red symbolizes health, strength and youth.

You haven't aged a day since 1938.

41

ADVENTURES OF SUPERMAN Nos. 559, 558 & 560

Opposite, above left and right: *Cover art, Tom Grummett and Dennis Rodier (inks on No. 559). June – August 1998.* A three-issue arc in *Adventures of Superman* sees the Man of Steel engaged in Silver Age shenanigans involving runaway comets and red kryptonite. A clever series of covers announced the retro change in tone, with a child's crayon drawing giving way to a classic "checkerboard" cover reminiscent of Curt Swan and finally a pencil layout done in the style of John Byrne.

9-11: THE WORLD'S FINEST WRITERS & ARTISTS TELL STORIES TO REMEMBER No. 2

Above: *Cover art, Alex Ross, 2002.* Alex Ross's painted cover was an homage to 1944's *Big All-American Comic Book.* Inside, writers and artists including Neil Gaiman, Brian K. Vaughan, Paul Pope, and Neal Adams honored the victims and heroes of the September 11, 2001, terrorist attacks.

BEHIND THE SCENES OF SUPERMAN RETURNS

Opposite: *Photograph, Brandon Routh as Superman and assistant during filming of a New Krypton sequence; director, Bryan Singer. 2006.*

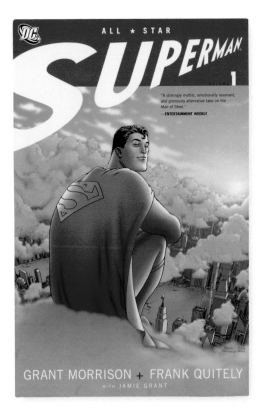

ALL STAR SUPERMAN No. 1

Above: *Cover art, Frank Quitely, January 2006.* In presenting
a Superman facing his own mortality, writer Grant Morrison
called up the best moments of the Man of Steel's long history,
including the menace of Doomsday and the Silver Age excess
of the Fortress of Solitude. Frank Quitely's expressive art
expertly conveyed a clumsy Clark, an easygoing Superman,
and a coldly lethal Lex Luthor.

SUPERMAN No. 204

Opposite: *Cover art, Jim Lee and Scott Williams, June 2004.*
A mirrored composition to Lee's cover for *Batman* No. 608, this
cover launched the "For Tomorrow" arc by *100 Bullets* writer
Brian Azzarello. The 12-part story sees Superman visit the
Phantom Zone and construct a new Fortress of Solitude in the
Peruvian jungle. When viewed against Lee's *Batman* cover,
this piece emphasizes the sunny art deco of Metropolis with
Superman's cape and stance indicating his readiness to leap
forward into action.

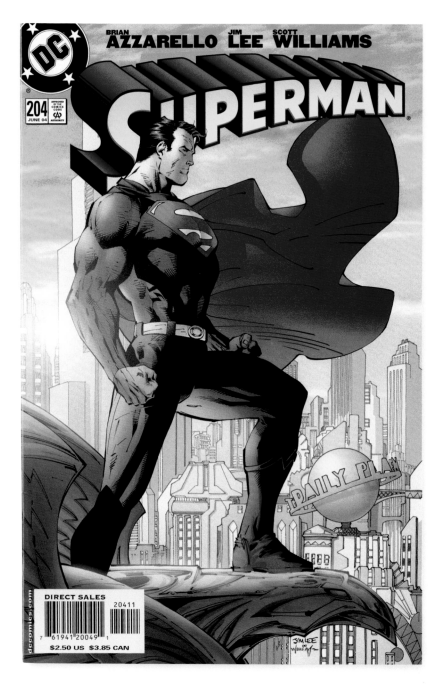

SUPERMAN: SECRET ORIGIN No. 3

Opposite: *Interior, "Mild-Mannered Reporter"; script, Geoff Johns; pencils, Gary Frank; inks, Jon Sibal. January 2010.* Superman's origin has often undergone small tweaks and big reboots, including *Man of Steel* and *Birthright*, but *Secret Origin* was the latest to nail down a definitive history for use within DC continuity. Told entirely from Clark's perspective, the six-part series eschewed Krypton flashbacks to focus on Clark's Kansas upbringing and his first experiences in Metropolis. Mixed in were elements from the *Smallville* television show and the first *Superman* film, including the nature of Clark's friendship with Lex Luthor and Lex's father, Lionel, plus bits of pre-*Crisis* history, such as the time-traveling visits by the Legion of Super Heroes.

SUPERMAN No. 700

Above: *Cover art, Gary Frank, August 2010.*

SUPERMAN No. 700

Below: *Cover art, Eduardo Risso, August 2010.* A tribute to Neal Adams's "Kryptonite Nevermore!" cover of *Superman* No. 233.

SUPERMAN: RED SON No. 2

Opposite: *Cover art, Dave Johnson, 2003.* "With his rigid notions of right and wrong, telescopic sight and super-hearing that can pick up a counter-revolutionary conversation half a world away, Superman becomes a terrifying global dictator, a nightmare fusion of Nietzsche's Übermensch and Orwell's Big Brother. If absolute power corrupts absolutely, superpower corrupts — well, even more." — *Time* magazine, 2004. In this Elseworlds tale by Mark Millar, Superman lands in Ukraine instead of Kansas, creating an alternate universe in which a prosperous Russia becomes the world's sole superpower and the U.S. (and its native genius Lex Luthor) a fractured, troublesome holdout.

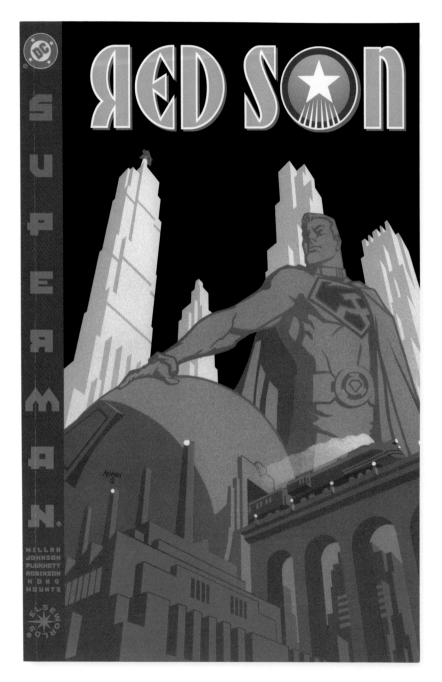

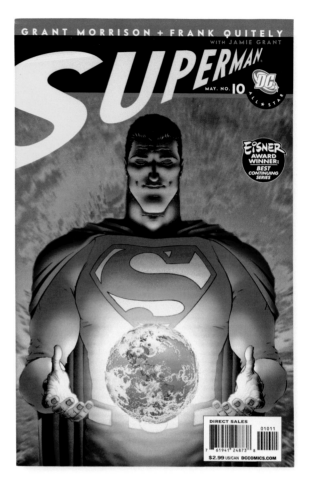

ALL STAR SUPERMAN No. 10

Opposite and above: *Original art and cover, Frank Quitely,
May 2008.* The 12 issues of *All Star Superman* begin with the
revelation that the Man of Steel is dying. His subsequent good
deeds reveal the bonds of friendship he forged with the *Daily
Planet* staff and the depth of his devotion to Lois, but by issue
No. 10 it's clear that Superman loves the entire Earth. The
cover by Frank Quitely began with simple pencils that changed
dramatically with final color and shading — emphasizing the
vulnerability of Superman's adopted planet and accentuating
a hint of a proud-parent smile. Color techniques had pro-
gressed mightily by the Modern Age.

SUPERMAN: PEACE ON EARTH

Above: *Cover art, Alex Ross, 1999.*

SUPERMAN No. 1 RE-CREATION

Opposite: *Warner Bros. Studio Stores lithograph, Alex Ross, 1998.*
One of the most famous comic covers of all time, *Superman*
No. 1 featured Joe Shuster's rendition of a watchful Man of
Steel suspended above his city. Ross re-created the image for
this lithograph, using his figure model Frank Kasy to help
capture Superman's pose and facial lighting, and expanding
the rooftops to create a background reminiscent of Berenice
Abbott's cityscape photos.

SUPERMAN: PEACE ON EARTH

Following spread: *Interior art, Alex Ross, 1999.*

THE BIG THREE IN YOUR POCKET

The Little Book of …
Batman
Superman
Wonder Woman

EDITORIAL NOTE

Early comics carried few credits or often credited creators of features rather than the actual talent producing the stories. We've endeavored to research credits for accuracy, and regret any errors.

This collection is based on material from the Eisner Award–winning *75 Years of DC Comics*, originally published in 2010 and the era-by-era volumes that followed.

The majority of the comics included in this series were photographed from the Ian Levine Collection. Also featured are the collections of Art Baltazar, Ivan M. Briggs, Saul Ferris, Grant Geissman, Tom Gordon, Jim Hambrick, P. C. Hamerlinck, Philip Hecht, Bob Joy, Chip Kidd, Peter Maresca, Jim Nolt, Jerry Robinson, David Saunders, Anthony Tollin, Ellen Vartanoff, Jerome Wenker, Mark Zaid, and, notably, Bob Bretall, Mark Waid, Heritage Auctions, and Metropolis Comics.

Any omissions for copy or credit are unintentional and appropriate credit will be given in future editions if such copyright holders contact the publisher.

DC STYLE GUIDE

Opposite: *Popular DC Super Heroes, art, José Luis García-López, 1982.*

SUPERMAN No. 24

Cover: *Cover art, Jack Burnley, September – October 1943.*

WORLD'S BEST COMICS No. 1

Page 2: *Cover art, Fred Ray, spring 1941.*

SUPERMAN No. 1 RE-CREATION

Back cover: *Warner Bros. Studio Stores lithograph, Alex Ross, 1998.*

EACH AND EVERY TASCHEN BOOK PLANTS A SEED!

TASCHEN is a carbon neutral publisher. Each year, we offset our annual carbon emissions with carbon credits at the Instituto Terra, a reforestation program in Minas Gerais, Brazil, founded by Lélia and Sebastião Salgado. To find out more about this ecological partnership, please check: *www.taschen.com/zerocarbon.*

INSPIRATION: UNLIMITED CARBON FOOTPRINT: ZERO.

To stay informed about TASCHEN and our upcoming titles, please subscribe to our free magazine at *www.taschen.com/ magazine,* follow us on Twitter, Instagram, and Facebook, or e-mail your questions to *contact@taschen.com.*

Editor, art direction, and design: Josh Baker, Oakland
Editorial consultants: Paul Levitz, Mark Waid, Martin Pasko, John Wells, and Daniel Wallace
Production: Stefan Klatte, Cologne
Layout: Nemuel DePaula, Los Angeles
Editorial coordination: Robert Noble, New York; Jascha Kempe, Cologne
Photography: Jennifer Patrick and Ed Fox, Los Angeles; Keith Krick, New York City
Spanish translation: Nuria Caminero Arranz for Delivering iBooks & Design, Barcelona
French translation: Alice Pétillot, Bordeaux

TASCHEN GMBH

Hohenzollernring 53, D-50672 Köln
www.taschen.com

Printed in China
ISBN 978-3-8365-7516-4
Not for individual resale

Thanks to Martin Pasko, Mark Waid, Daniel Wallace, and especially John Wells for research and writing assistance on captions and biographies.

Special thanks to Ian Levine for allowing access to his amazing collection. Thanks as well to Bob Bretall, who holds the 2014 Guinness World Record for Largest Collection of Comic Books and freely allowed us to dive into his trove.

At DC Comics, thanks are due to Michael Acampora, Allan Asherman, Karen Berger, Roger Bonas, Georg Brewer, Richard Bruning, Mike Carlin, Christopher Cerasi, Mark Chiarello, Eddy Choi, Ivan Cohen, Dan DiDio, John Ficarra, Larry Ganem, Bob Harras, Geoff Johns, Bob Joy, Hank Kanalz, Kevin Kiniry, Jay Kogan, Jim Lee, Evan Metcalf, Connor Michel, Lisa Mills, John Morgan, Diane Nelson, Scott Nybakken, Anthony Palumbo, Frank Pittarese, Barbara Rich, Cheryl Rubin, Andrea Shochet, Joe Siegel, Bob Wayne, Scott Bryan Wilson, Michael Wooten, and Dora Yoshimoto. At Warner Bros., my thanks to Josh Anderson, Leith Adams, Ben Harper, Stephanie Mente, and Nikolas Primack.

Many thanks to the numerous individuals who helped in the production of this series of books, including Jack Adler; Doug Adrianson; Teena Apeles; Dawn Arrington; Chris Bailey; Jerry Bails; Art Baltazar; John Barton; Jerry Beck; John Benson; Steve Bingen; Arnold Blumberg; Brian Bolland; Jim Bowers; Cindy Brenner; Ivan Briggs; Jonathan Browne; Scott Byers; Steve Carey; PeteCarlsson; Mildred Champlin; Dale Cendali; Ruth Clampett; Alice Cloos; Dick Cole; Wesley Coller; Gerry Conway; Margaret Croft; Les Daniels; Dave Davis; Jack Davis; Ken DellaPenta; Joe Desris; Lee Dillon; Michael Doret; Spencer Douglas; Paul Duncan; Mallory Farrugia; Saul Ferris; Stephen Fishler; Chaz Fitzhugh; Steve Fogelson; Danny Fuchs; Neil Gaiman; Craig B. Gaines; Grant Geissman; Dave Gibbons; Frank Goerhardt; Tom Gordon; Steven P. Gorman; Jared Green; Steven Grossfeld; James Halperin; Jim Hambrick; P. C. Hamerlinck; Yadira Harrison; Chuck Harter; Philip Hecht; Jim Heimann; Joseph Heller; Andy Hershberger; Jessica Hoffman; Martin Holz; Julia Howe; Adam Hyman; Lisa Janney; Klaus Janson; Jenette Kahn; Elizabeth Kane; Chip Kidd; Kirk Kimball; Denis and Stacy Kitchen; Stefan Klatte; Todd Klein; Florian Kobler; Charles Kochman; Christopher Kosek; Keith Krick; Joe Kubert; Danny Kuchuck; Amy Kule; PaulKupperberg; Olive Lamotte; Caroline Lee; Hannah and Alfred Levitz; Jeanette, Nicole, Philip, and Garret Levitz; Steven Lomazow; Alice and Leonard Maltin; Tony Manzella; Peter Maresca; Byrne Marston; Pete Marston; Rachel Maximo; David Mazzucchelli; Thea Miklowski; John Morrow; Mark McKenna; Ryann McQuilton; Eric Nash; Constantine Nasr; Meike Niessen; Scott Neitlich; Adam Newell; Maggie Nimkin; Robert Noble; Mark Nobleman; Jim Nolt; Erica Pak; Jennifer Patrick; Kirstin Plate; Joe Orlando; Joe Rainone; Debbie Rexing; Dennis Robert; Jerry Robinson; Alex Ross; Barry Sandoval; Mike Sangiacomo; David Saunders; Zina Saunders; Randy Scott; Susannah Scott; Jürgen Seidel; David Siegel; John Smedley; Ben Smith; Wayne Smith; Geoff Spear; Art Spiegelman; Bob Stein; Roy Thomas; Shane Thompson; Anthony Tollin; Jessica Trujillo; Ellen Vartanoff; Mark Voglesong; Mike Voiles; Phillip Wages; Chris Ware; William Wasson; Evan Weinerman; Jerry Weist; Sean Welch; Jerome Wenker; Josh White; Douglas Wheeler-Nicholson; Nicky Wheeler-Nicholson; Alex Winter; DebbySue Wolfcale; Marv Wolfman; Steve Younis; Mark Zaid; Thomas Zellers; Barry Ziehl; Marco Zivny; and Vincent Zurzolo.

And a special acknowledgment to Steve Korté, Josh Baker, and Nina Wiener, and the eagle eye of Benedikt Taschen, without whom this series of books would have been impossible.

— **PAUL LEVITZ**

SUPERMAN